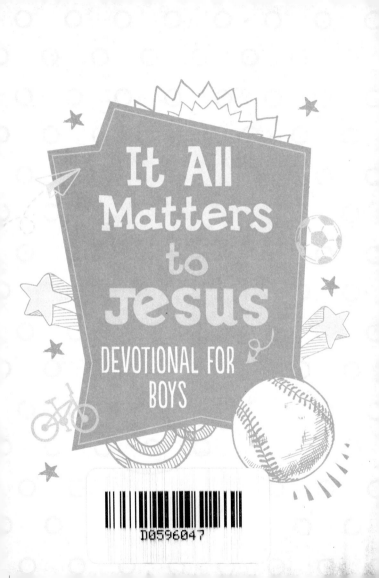

It All Matters to Jesus

DEVOTIONAL FOR BOYS

D0596047

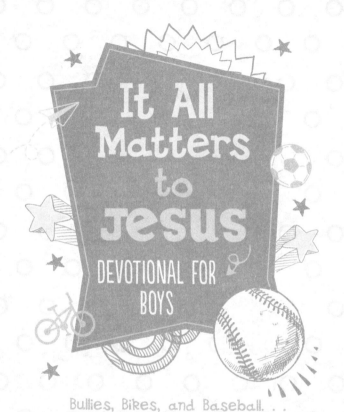

It All Matters to JESUS

DEVOTIONAL FOR BOYS

Bullies, Bikes, and Baseball. . .
He Cares about It All!

GLENN HASCALL

BARBOUR BOOKS
An Imprint of Barbour Publishing, Inc.

Published by Barbour Books, an imprint of Barbour Publishing, Inc., P.O. Box 719, Uhrichsville, Ohio 44683, www.barbourbooks.com

Our mission is to publish and distribute inspirational products offering exceptional value and biblical encouragement to the masses.

ECPA Member of the
Evangelical Christian
Publishers Association

Printed in the United States of America.
05301 0216 DP

CONTENTS

Introduction..7

Chapter 1—Hey, What's Your Name?.....................9

Chapter 2—The Joy of a Softened Heart................15

Chapter 3—The Perfect Action Plan....................21

Chapter 4—Better Choice This Time....................27

Chapter 5—The Good, the Bad, and the Smelly........33

Chapter 6—Doing the Right Thing.....................39

Chapter 7—Honesty—the Unexpected Choice............45

Chapter 8—An Undeniable Influence 51

Chapter 9—The Liberal Use of Word Glue..............57

Chapter 10—The Work Gets Done 63

Chapter 11—Failing at God's Job......................69

Chapter 12—Bad Day Survival Guide...................75

Chapter 13—Better Days Ahead........................81

Chapter 14—Embracing God's Big Idea 87

Chapter 15—Gus Finds His Courage 93

Chapter 16—How Did You Get That?...................99

Chapter 17—Welcome to the Grown-Up Table.........105

Chapter 18—One Choice Changes Who You Are......111

Chapter 19—No Subtraction on Maple Lane...........117

Chapter 20—Integrity Boot Camp.....................123

Chapter 21—The Honorable Truth .129

Chapter 22—Honor in the Family Tree 135

Chapter 23—Humility in a "Me First" World. 141

Chapter 24—Bully in the Hall 147

Chapter 25—Acknowledging the Existence of

Emotional Control 153

Chapter 26—When Manners Surprise and Amaze 159

Chapter 27—The Heart to Run 165

Chapter 28—Hold On: This Could Get Brilliant 171

Chapter 29—Transformed by Obedience 177

Chapter 30—The Fellowship of the Rejected. 183

Chapter 31—You're Not Alone. 189

Chapter 32—God Time—Any Time. 195

Chapter 33—A Time to Turn Around. 201

Chapter 34—The Seeking-Finding-Learning-Following

Principle. 206

Chapter 35—The Neglected List of Wants. 212

Chapter 36—Whatcha Thinkin'? 218

Chapter 37—Time to Handle the Truth 224

Chapter 38—Some Stuff Is Just That Important 230

Chapter 39—The Electronic Discussion 236

Chapter 40—It Won't Be Long 242

Scripture Index. 249

How is it possible to pick just 40 topics that matter to Jesus? Honestly, we tried. Since everything matters to Jesus, we decided to choose 40 things that should also matter to you. After all, if it matters to Jesus, it should matter to us, right?

This book is the result of months of research, writing, and review. We wanted this to be just right for the issues you face every day. Things like compassion, attitude, worry, generosity, integrity, obedience, prayer, our thoughts, and wisdom. We'll find out why it matters and what the Bible says about it.

Spend time here and consider some pretty important information. When things that matter to Jesus also matter to us, we can help others see how Jesus changes lives, helps us understand, and gives our lives new purpose. He never leaves us without direction.

You'll also see the things that matter to us bring about the compassion and patience of God.

It all matters to Jesus—and Jesus should matter to us.

CHAPTER 1
HEY, WHAT'S YOUR NAME?

At family gatherings people tell stories. You might hear about something your grandpa did when he was young or a fish that got away on a trip to a nearby creek. You may not have been alive when the stories happened, but the names of those who lived them become important when you share the stories with others.

Names are important. A first name is personal and helps others see you as unique. A last name points to the family you come from. A middle name? . . . Well, that can be a name you like, loathe, or forget. Sometimes you only hear your middle name when you've done something wrong. When your entire name is spoken, it usually means you need to pay attention to an important message— usually from a family member.

Jesus had many names. He was called Prophet, Teacher, Friend, Savior, and Son of God. Each name helped people understand Him better but also showed how others viewed Him. For instance, someone who called Him Teacher didn't know Him nearly as well as someone who called Him Son of God.

You have special names, too. Some might call you Smart, Talented, Trustworthy, or even Son, Grandson, or Nephew. You might be Neighbor, Friend, Classmate, or Student. Not all people will call you by these special names. For instance, you wouldn't expect your best friend to call you Grandson. This is a special name only your grandparents would use. On the other hand, your grandparents probably wouldn't call you Classmate. Your teacher could use many names such as Smart, Talented, Trustworthy, and Student. On a bad day, other names might apply.

People you see in school have names. Some you know, a few you use, and some you might need to learn. More than just names, these people can carry labels such as Kind, Funny, Friendly, Stuck-Up, and Bully, along with more labels than we can print. Not all labels are good. Not all labels are true. And not all labels should be used.

When we show honor in the way we use names, we're telling other people that we see them as valuable. Showing respect helps other people see you as friendly, and they will be less cautious when talking to you. Friendships can only grow when you trust the other person—and they trust you.

Our actions have names like Love, Joy, Peace, Patience, Kindness, Goodness, Faithfulness, Gentleness, and Self-Control (see Galatians 5:22–23). To have someone use these names to describe you is a real compliment, it pleases God, and this type of name-calling is never against the law.

. . . .

Do not be misled:
"Bad company corrupts good character."
1 CORINTHIANS 15:33 NIV

. . . .

People we call friends should be encouraged by our lives, and we should be encouraged by their faith. Everybody needs friends, but some people will only encourage you to do things that have never pleased God.

God invented relationships. He never wants us to try to live in a way that keeps us apart from people. Because it matters to Jesus, we have to learn the value of friendships, the choices that inspire friendships, and the heart that welcomes friendships even when the idea of introducing ourselves scares us.

Friends are known for their compassion and for wanting to know us well enough that trust becomes a two-way street. Jesus had this kind of friendship with most of His disciples, and He's always shown that if you have real friends, you have an impressive treasure.

When we show compassion, we're saying that other people are important to us. We care about them and want to help them. This is why friendship is something all of us need. This is why being a friend is something we all should be. It's also why we understand the power of names and use them wisely.

Be the friend God wants you to be by doing what He asks you to do.

· ·

[Jesus said,] "You are my friends
if you do what I command."

JOHN 15:14

· ·

Friendships Matter. . . .

★ Jesus wants us to have friends and be friendly.

★ Good friends are people we can trust.

★ Good friends are a gift, not something you buy.

★ Good friends don't give up.

★ Meeting new people can be scary.

★ Not everyone who wants a friend will act like it.

★ You don't have to wait to be introduced to someone to start a friendship.

★ Jesus wants to be our friend.

★ Names are important.

★ God knows your name.

You saw me before I was born.
Every day of my life was recorded in your book.
Every moment was laid out
before a single day had passed.
PSALM 139:16

THE JOY OF A SO

To sculpt
and dire
but

Ben looked forward to learning
class. He wanted to use clay to c
beautiful. If not beautiful, then at
He could do that. Right? When the   ...ally
arrived, each student was handed a plastic
tub of modeling clay. One by one the students
squeezed the clay and began to roll and shape
their masterpieces (most looked like earthworms
with pimples). Ben was the last person to get a tub
of clay. He opened the lid and tried to push his
thumb into the mixture. Instead of soft clay, the
contents of his tub were hard. That's when Ben
noticed the crack in the container. Outside air had
dried the clay and made it unusable. All he could
offer with his clay was a reddish-colored hockey
puck, paperweight, or possibly an abstract, yet
featureless, duck. The clay had set so it couldn't
be molded. If Ben wanted success as a sculptor, he
would need soft clay.

...eans someone influences the shape
...ion of the clay. People do that with clay,
...od does it with people.

O Lord, you are our Father.
We are the clay, and you are the potter.
We all are formed by your hand.
ISAIAH 64:8

If you have some time and it's okay with your
family, go outside and look around at everything
that wasn't built by a human being. This includes
the sky, grass, flowers, squirrels, pets, birds, ponds,
fish, and any wild muskrat, loon, or cricket that
passes by.

God made all of it, and He made the materials
humans use to make everything else. God also
made you. Psalm 139 says He fashioned us in our
mother's womb. It's okay to think of this as God
sculpting us.

*For we are God's masterpiece. He has created
us anew in Christ Jesus, so we can do the
good things he planned for us long ago.*
EPHESIANS 2:10

There are five words in this verse that are worth
looking at again—*He has created us anew*. The
God who sculpted our body can turn us into a
masterpiece when we allow Him to soften and
resculpt our heart. When we accept God's great
rescue plan known as *salvation*, we take the first
step in allowing Him to make *all* things new, and it
starts in the heart and mind.

When Jesus reshapes, it changes who we are,
what we do, and how we speak. We will be more
interested in His plan, other people, and following
directions. Where it was easy to hate others before,
our heart will be more interested in forgiveness
and love. That's just the beginning of the changes
brought on by His resculpting.

Jesus saved us, He is remaking us, and old
things will get left behind. This includes a hard

heart that can't change on its own. Our attitudes will undergo a change, and so will our actions.

"And I will give you a new heart, and I will put a new spirit in you. I will take out your stony, stubborn heart and give you a tender, responsive heart."
EZEKIEL 36:26

It's easy to make choices that help us. We work to be first in line, last to help, and invisible to those who annoy us. We want what we want, how we want it, and at the moment we see it. This is why Jesus works to reshape how we think. When we cooperate with "the Potter," we'll learn to want what He wants, how He wants it, and at the moment He wants it. It's called transformation, and it really means to change from one person into another—with the expert help of Jesus.

Ben may have had trouble softening the clay he was trying to use for class, but Jesus can always soften a heart that's willing to change. Jesus is taking something that's already amazing—you!—

and turning it into a masterpiece. You were born with special skills, interests, and personality. When God's done with you, He can use you to help change the world.

Your Heart Matters. . . .

★ God made you.

★ Jesus wants to reshape your heart so it's more like His.

★ Jesus' rescue plan—salvation—completes what God calls a "masterpiece."

★ Jesus wants us to leave old things behind.

★ When Jesus reshapes our heart, it will change who we are, what we do, and how we speak.

★ A soft heart makes us more interested in other people.

★ God can use you to help change the world.

★ Jesus wants each of us to have beautiful hearts.

★ A reshaped heart changes your attitude.

- ★ Jesus can soften any willing heart.
- ★ A hard heart is a selfish heart.
- ★ A soft heart is a giving heart.
- ★ Jesus reshapes the way we think about what we want.

Anyone who belongs to Christ
has become a new person.
The old life is gone; a new life has begun!
2 CORINTHIANS 5:17

CHAPTER 3
THE PERFECT ACTION PLAN

Wyatt wondered if anything would ever go right. It's not like he hadn't planned out what he wanted to do. He had a notebook filled with the things he wanted to accomplish, but he'd had very few successes. There weren't very many check marks on his list. He felt ready to give up and wondered if success was a myth.

Goals were important, weren't they? Wyatt saw kids every day who had no idea what they would be when they were adults. Wyatt knew—or thought he did. He had a motivational poster in his room that read, "Success invites friends—get prepared for the good life." He didn't know who wrote it, but as he read it once more he thought the writer had no idea what he or she was talking about. Maybe it was time for a new poster.

Jesus said, "Come to me, all of you who are weary and carry heavy burdens, and I will give you rest. Take my yoke upon you. Let me teach you, because I am humble and gentle at heart, and you will find rest for your souls. For my yoke is easy to bear, and the burden I give you is light."

MATTHEW 11:28–30

When Jesus spoke of a yoke, the people who heard would have understood. A younger horse, ox, or cow would be partnered with the same type of work animal that helped on a farm. The yoke was a type of harness that fit over the necks of both animals if they stood side by side. The younger and less experienced animal wouldn't know what to do and would try to run away. However, because it was connected to the experienced animal, it couldn't go anywhere without its work partner. It didn't take long for the younger animal to learn how to do the work. The yoke was a training tool.

Jesus offers to teach us in a similar way. We

don't know everything, but sometimes we act like we do. Jesus invites us to be yoked with Him. We can pull and tug, but if we're patient, we'll begin to understand that Jesus leads and we follow. When we relax, we begin to see the things Jesus always does, the things He never does, and the things He wants us to do.

Jesus tells us to *come to Him*. He won't force us to walk with Him but invites us to enjoy His company.

Jesus knows we are *weary and carry heavy burdens*. He knows we need assistance, and He's willing to help.

Jesus offers *rest*. He knows we get tired trying to make sense of everything. He has things figured out, which is why we can relax.

Jesus invites us to *let Him teach*. Being yoked with Jesus helps us learn to follow directions.

Jesus says His *burden is light*. This is because He does the hard work. We just need to walk with Him.

If we don't know what Jesus wants us to do, then it's easy to see why most of our plans fail. When we don't know that Jesus has an action plan for us, then the best we can do is guess. That's like taking a test we've never studied for. We might get a few answers right, but it's not because we actually knew. The end result of this strategy is failure, but it's not that we didn't try. Maybe we just didn't know.

We become yoked with Jesus when we learn what He said and do what He taught. If Jesus provides an example, then follow it. If He gives a command, then obey it. If He provides a warning, then pay attention. He's willing to teach you, but you have to choose to be His student.

Training is the next step after accepting God's rescue plan, but many people never choose to get in the yoke with Jesus. They treat Him more like a guidance counselor that they talk to from time to time.

There's nothing wrong with making plans, but when you let Jesus lead, be prepared to move in a new direction. Proverbs 16:9 says, "We can make our plans, but the LORD determines our steps."

Who chooses your steps?

Training Matters. . . .

★ We don't know everything, but sometimes we act like we do.

★ If we're patient, we'll begin to understand that Jesus leads and we follow.

★ Jesus won't force us to walk with Him, but He invites us to enjoy His company.

★ Jesus knows we need assistance, and He's willing to help.

★ Jesus has things figured out, which is why we can relax.

★ Being yoked with Jesus helps us follow His directions.

★ Jesus does the hard work. We just need to walk with Him.

★ Jesus provides examples for us to follow.

★ Jesus gives commands for us to obey.

★ Jesus gives us warnings about things to avoid.

★ Training is the next step after we accept God's rescue plan of salvation.

*Your word is a lamp to guide
my feet and a light for my path.*

PSALM 119:105

CHAPTER 4
BETTER CHOICE THIS TIME

Steve helped his dad build a doghouse for their favorite pooch, Porkchop. He'd never done anything like it before and was surprised at how good he felt working with tools from his dad's workbench. Steve was just a couple of hammer swings away from finishing the roof when the head of the hammer came in contact with the nail of his thumb. Warning sirens filled his mind, and Steve did his best imitation of caveman yodeling and Bigfoot attempting to dance. At least Porkchop seemed impressed.

You can be sure Steve will do everything he can to avoid hitting his thumb again because no one likes caveman yodeling or the dance moves of Sasquatch.

When we break God's law, it can feel a bit like hitting our thumb with a hammer. God can get our attention, make us uncomfortable, and then He willingly forgives and heals the pain of our wounds.

God gives us consequences for sin so we can remember why we shouldn't do it again. Forgiveness should never be considered a reward for bad behavior. God forgives us so we're encouraged to live for Him, walk with Him, and voluntarily choose to obey His commands.

Some people want to believe that because God is willing to forgive they have no need to obey. Some have even said, "It's easier to ask for forgiveness than permission." This thinking is not at all what God had in mind when Jesus paid for every sin of humankind. The gift Jesus gave was expensive.

Without the shedding of blood,
there is no forgiveness.
HEBREWS 9:22

Jesus had to die for us to be forgiven.

Does that sound like a common gift?

When you accept Jesus' rescue plan, you should remember it was this priceless gift that gave us the freedom to talk to God. Knowing this might make you think you aren't worthy enough to even ask for forgiveness, but you should never think that. Jesus wants to forgive you, and you need to be forgiven. By remembering what it took to make forgiveness available, you might just learn to be more careful with the choices you make.

Jesus lets us use His forgiveness anytime we need it, but He'd be happier accepting your gift of obedience. We can never become more like Jesus if we stay in a place where obedience is unfamiliar to us. Jesus loved us enough to forgive, so we should love Him enough to obey.

If you find that disobeying your parents means you lose a privilege, you are more likely to obey when the same issue comes up again. If you have to stay after school because you failed to complete an assignment in class, you'll probably be more willing to complete the next assignment on time. If you find that disobeying God keeps you from Him, then you'll want to admit your sin and ask His forgiveness. You'll probably make better choices in the future because you have firsthand experience with disobedience and the pain it causes.

Whom did Jesus come to rescue?

"Healthy people don't need a doctor—sick people do. I have come to call not those who think they are righteous, but those who know they are sinners."

MARK 2:17

Recognizing you disobeyed God is the first step in knowing where to go for forgiveness—Jesus.

Did Jesus really tell us not to sin? To one man Jesus said, "Stop sinning" (see John 5:14). To a woman he said, "Go and sin no more" (see John 8:11).

Jesus came to rescue you from sin. He is clear that His rescue plan includes forgiveness. He is clear that obedience leads to positive change in your life. He is clear that the positive change in your life will show other people what His forgiveness can do for them.

*But if we confess our sins to him, he is
faithful and just to forgive us our sins and
to cleanse us from all wickedness.*

1 JOHN 1:9

Forgiveness Matters. . . .

★ All people sin.

★ Sin requires forgiveness.

★ There are consequences for sin.

★ The gift of forgiveness cost Jesus everything.

★ Forgiveness is not a common gift.

★ Jesus wants to forgive.

★ You need to be forgiven.

★ Jesus wants us to make our choices wisely.

★ Obedience makes us more like Jesus.

★ Sin keeps God at a distance.

★ Others see the change Jesus makes in people
when they obey.

I don't mean to say that I have already achieved these things or that I have already reached perfection. But I press on to possess that perfection for which Christ Jesus first possessed me. No, dear brothers and sisters, I have not achieved it, but I focus on this one thing: Forgetting the past and looking forward to what lies ahead, I press on to reach the end of the race and receive the heavenly prize for which God, through Christ Jesus, is calling us.

PHILIPPIANS 3:12–14

CHAPTER 5

THE GOOD, THE BAD, AND THE SMELLY

Spencer has an unusual habit. Before he goes to bed, he takes off his socks, holds them up to his nose, and sniffs deeply. The habit started when he was really little and everyone thought it was cute. Spencer's mom even has pictures and videos of his sock sniffing. His older sister Kelly has only one word for the habit: *gross*. This may not be a good or bad habit but maybe a habit that's not helpful.

It takes awhile to grow into a new habit. It's like planting a seed. It may take some time to go from seed to a habit harvest. If it's a good habit, then keep working at it even on hard days. If it's a bad habit, pull it out by the roots—the sooner, the better.

You say, "I am allowed to do anything"—
but not everything is good for you.
And even though "I am allowed to do anything,"
I must not become a slave to anything.

1 CORINTHIANS 6:12

Good habits are action plans that demonstrate you're willing to follow God's commands. Bad habits are actions and activities that go against God's commands and are called sin because they break God's law. There are additional bad habits that just aren't healthy or wise. There are some habits that are unique to you, and you've never really been able to figure out if they're good or bad.

One of the easiest ways to know if a habit is bad is if you spend most of your time participating in the habit. If what you're doing takes time away from God, family, or school, then even activities that may be okay for you to be involved in can be bad. Why? The habit no longer makes it possible for you to find a balance between your habit and everything else you should be doing.

For instance, if you say, "I'd spend more time reading the Bible, but I've got this video game that I'm real close to beating," then you may have moved from an activity that might have been acceptable in your family to a habit that is no longer helpful because it's no longer in balance.

Good habits will always put God and others first. If your habit has to do with learning more about God and following His plan, then you can be sure it's a good habit.

Don't copy the behavior and customs of this world, but let God transform you into a new person by changing the way you think. Then you will learn to know God's will for you, which is good and pleasing and perfect.

Romans 12:2

The life choices of a Christian will probably seem different from others. If we act just like everyone else and do things just like them, then how will others see that God has changed us? If God really changes us, then we will be different. We won't just be different when we're at church or with Christian friends. The thing that makes us different—Jesus—will be invited everywhere we go. Jesus will help us learn what should change and how to live a generous, overflowing, and abundant life.

The less like the world you are, the clearer God's plan becomes. If you refuse to let God change the way you think, then it's really hard for you to understand what He wants. Psalm 111:10 says, "All who obey his commandments will grow in wisdom." Obedience to God's plan always comes before wisdom.

If habits had a smell, then some of them would smell worse than Spencer's socks after gym class. On the other hand, there might be some habits that have a pretty great smell—the kind that pleases God. Take the time to learn God's plan, follow His directions, and show the world that obedience to God can make anyone wise.

Get wisdom; develop good judgment. Don't forget my words or turn away from them.

PROVERBS 4:5

Habits Matter. . . .

★ New habits take time to grow.

★ Get rid of bad habits and replace them with good ones.

★ Good habits demonstrate a willingness to follow God's commands.

★ Choices to disobey God's commands are called sin and can become habits.

★ Our worst habits will cause us to spend less time learning from God.

★ Our best habits put God and others first.

★ If you refuse to let God change the way you think, then it's really hard for you to understand what He wants.

★ Obeying God is always the first step to becoming wise.

★ Some habits are not helpful because they keep us from God.

★ Learn God's plan, follow His directions, and show others that obedience to God can make anyone wise.

*If you are wise and understand God's ways,
prove it by living an honorable life, doing good
works with the humility that comes from wisdom.*

JAMES 3:13

CHAPTER 6
DOING THE RIGHT THING

Kenny had a forest just beyond his back gate. He and his friends played among the trees after school. They even had a clubhouse in one of the large trees. One day Kenny spotted a wooden handle resting on a tree root. The rest of the mysterious tool was buried in dead leaves. He tugged on the handle and discovered a leaf rake. Now they could clean out the area around their clubhouse, and they did. The oddest thing about the rake was that a metal spoon had been attached. It didn't help with raking, and none of Kenny's friends could figure out why it was there.

The next day Kenny talked with all his neighbors to see if they had lost a rake. None had. Kenny's dad told him if no one claimed the rake in thirty days, it was his. To Kenny, this rake was his forest treasure, and he couldn't wait to claim it as his own. On the thirty-first day, he did.

Some people say that *character* is a word you

use to describe someone's personality, but that may not go quite far enough. Character is a set of beliefs and actions that may only show up when you have hard choices to make.

Rick had been taught that stealing was wrong. He'd been wanting a tablet computer for months. Rick spotted a man at a park leaving his tablet behind. Would it be stealing to take something someone just left? Could he justify his actions, saying God caused the man to leave it because He knew how much Rick wanted one? What would Rick's character allow him to do?

If Rick had always believed stealing was wrong but his character accepted a "finders keepers" perspective, then his character might prove that under certain circumstances Rick felt stealing was all right.

God's answer?

"Do not steal. Do not deceive or cheat one another."
LEVITICUS 19:11

Sometimes we're never sure what choices we'll make until faced with making that choice quickly. We might make a decision we never thought we would make. Why? Most of us never make a decision about how we'll respond before we actually have to make the decision. We haven't decided we won't ever steal and then face a decision to take something that would be easy to steal. We haven't chosen to be responsible, and then we're asked to be responsible. We haven't decided to be honest, and then we're tempted to lie. Wrong choices often follow.

Jesus wants to build character in our lives. He wants us to think about and make decisions affecting what our future character looks like. If we want to be honest in the future, we need to do two things: (1) be honest today and (2) decide that honesty will always be our choice.

Waiting to make a decision about God's issues will often leave you in a place where you're tempted to make a wrong choice.

The temptations in your life are no different from
what others experience. And God is faithful. He will
not allow the temptation to be more than you can
stand. When you are tempted, he will show you a
way out so that you can endure.

1 CORINTHIANS 10:13

In the case of character, the easiest way out of temptation is to already know the right answer and then make the right choice.

Kenny's story isn't quite done yet. He'd waited a month before claiming the rake. He'd done the right thing, but a knock on the door left Kenny with a new choice. An older woman he'd never seen stood smiling on the steps of his house. He listened to her story of the missing rake. It had been a gift from her husband many years before he'd passed away. He'd put the spoon on the rake so she could dig small plants in the forest and bring them home. The rake wasn't worth much and she could buy another, but the spoon rake meant something to her because it always reminded her of how much her husband loved her.

What do you think Kenny did? What would you do? Why?

Character Matters. . . .

★ Character is a set of beliefs and actions that are proven when making hard choices.

★ Jesus wants our character to look like His.

★ When we don't develop character, it's easier to make wrong choices.

★ Jesus wants to be our character builder.

★ Waiting to make a decision about following God's way will always leave you tempted to make wrong choices.

★ Jesus wants us to think about and make decisions affecting what our future character looks like.

★ The easiest way out of temptation is to already know the right answer.

★ The easiest way to move past temptation is to make the right choice.

★ Character is a set of beliefs and choices you make before temptation shows up uninvited.

Choose a good reputation over great riches; being held in high esteem is better than silver or gold.

PROVERBS 22:1

CHAPTER 7
HONESTY—
THE UNEXPECTED CHOICE

Alex was the first person in Mr. Schneider's classroom. This was the morning of the *big test*. He had studied for more than a week but was still not sure he knew the answer to every question. Alex had heard kids talking about the ways they planned to pass the test. Some planned to study, but others looked for ways to get the answer without studying. Alex had come to a personal understanding that this decision was cheating, but most of his friends thought it was just finding a "competitive edge."

It wasn't so long ago that Alex had felt the same way. He'd seen the news about sports heroes using performance-enhancing drugs to beat their opponents. He'd read about people in business who had taken money from people they couldn't pay back. Alex knew one thing for sure: the last time he cheated, he was caught. He also knew that he wouldn't have heard about the athletes

and business owners if they hadn't been caught.
Cheaters are eventually discovered.

*People with integrity walk safely, but those
who follow crooked paths will be exposed.*
PROVERBS 10:9

What causes a person to cheat? Cheating is often
viewed as a shortcut to finding success. If you
cheat but the end result is a better grade, higher
position, or more awards, then you may feel the act
of cheating allowed you to gain an advantage over
others. God has a different perspective: "Don't lie to
each other, for you have stripped off your old sinful
nature and all its wicked deeds" (Colossians 3:9).

Cheating is a lie that may never be spoken. It's
being quietly deceitful, hoping others don't catch
on. Cheating is extremely selfish.

When you cheat on a test, you want a grade
you didn't earn. When you cheat by not doing what
you told your parents you would, you take time and
effort that belonged to your family. When you cheat

in sports, you want others to think you're better than you are.

There are three ways to tell if you are cheating:
1. You don't follow rules and look for ways to make what you need to do easier.
2. You take something that doesn't belong to you by lying and deceiving others.
3. You make sure other people who have worked hard don't get what they deserve by taking the credit for yourself.

It shouldn't surprise us when people try to convince us they aren't cheating when they're caught in the act. Because cheating involves lying, it can become really easy to continue lying even after you're caught.

Jesus said to the people who believed in him, "You are truly my disciples if you remain faithful to my teachings. And you will know the truth, and the truth will set you free."
JOHN 8:31-32

To remain faithful to what Jesus taught is to say that everything He said matters. He loved people and helped them. He honored those who gave generously and confronted those who cheated.

Jesus wants us to be content with what He gives us and satisfied with the choices we make. Cheating shows we're not satisfied with His gifts and that we're willing to make bad decisions in order to take ownership of something He may not have wanted us to have.

It almost comes as a surprise to people when they discover someone who is honest. Some seem to believe sin is the most obvious first choice. However, we have to live with each choice we make. When we admit our sin, God forgives every time. Because we should desire to obey Him, we're less interested in making bad choices. The memories of sin are nothing to be proud of.

It wasn't long ago when Alex sat in class and felt it was unfair that so many students cheated and got away with it. The longer he thought about it, the more convinced he was that it made sense to cheat. He felt there were more interesting things he could do with his time than to study. Mr. Schneider caught him and immediately gave him a failing grade on the test. Alex was faced with extra homework assignments, detention, and plenty of quality time with Mr. Schneider. These consequences helped Alex readjust his thinking and regain the trust of his teacher.

Truth Matters. . . .

★ Cheating is sometimes viewed as a way to succeed.

★ Cheating is quietly deceiving other people.

★ Cheaters break rules to make their lives easier.

★ Cheaters are eventually caught.

★ Truthful people keep rules and follow Jesus.

★ Cheaters take things that don't belong to them.

★ Truthful people give things that help others.

★ Cheaters seek to be honored.

★ Truthful people point to Jesus, who is most honorable.

★ Jesus wants us to be content with what He gives us and satisfied with the choices we make.

★ Jesus knows that as we obey Him, we're less interested in making bad choices.

Stand your ground, putting on the belt of truth and the body armor of God's righteousness.
EPHESIANS 6:14

CHAPTER 8
AN UNDENIABLE INFLUENCE

Everyone thought Joe was going to do something special with his life. Teachers liked him, he was popular but still treated others well, and Joe was pretty good at almost. . .everything. That was before Joe met Austin, who was a year older, full of anger, and seemed to be the leader of the Bad Decisions Club. Austin lacked respect for others, thought Jesus was a joke, and believed laws were meant for weak people.

At first Joe just observed what Austin did, but time wore him down. He dipped his toe in the deep end of poor choices, and it wasn't long before his life bore the marks of time spent with Austin.

Don't befriend angry people or associate with hot-tempered people, or you will learn to be like them and endanger your soul.
PROVERBS 22:24–25

We begin to act like the people we spend the most time with. God invites us to love everyone but wants us to spend more time with Christians than those who don't follow Him. This isn't punishment for the non-Christian, but safety for us. It is easier for a person who makes poor choices to influence a Christian than for a Christian to influence someone who sees no reason to change his or her decision-making process.

We're influenced by the opinions of others. They can influence us to make good choices, or they can suggest a path that puts us at a distance from others, which leads to choices we'll regret. Sometimes we worry too much about the approval of the wrong person.

I'm not trying to win the approval of people, but of God. If pleasing people were my goal, I would not be Christ's servant.
GALATIANS 1:10

If we really want to live for Jesus, there may be people we can't hang out with as much as we want. They may disrespect our choice to follow Jesus. A Christian is commanded to love, but non-Christians don't live by God's commands. They may like breaking God's law.

No one wants to be made fun of, so it's tempting to excuse our choice to follow Jesus. It isn't long before we're making fun of Jesus right along with those who won't encourage our walk with Jesus. How did we get to the place where we're making choices we thought we'd never make?

* *

Don't be fooled. . .for "bad company corrupts good character."
1 CORINTHIANS 15:33

* *

The book of Proverbs is filled with wisdom about life, relationships, and God. Think about what it has to say about friends.

Bad Friends

With their words, the godless destroy their friends.
PROVERBS 11:9

Young people who obey the law are wise;
those with wild friends bring shame to their parents.
PROVERBS 28:7

Good Friends

The godly give good advice to their friends;
the wicked lead them astray.
PROVERBS 12:26

A friend is always loyal, and a
brother is born to help in time of need.
PROVERBS 17:17

Jesus wants us to build good friendships. He can use those friendships to help us when we need help. Bad friendships don't seem to care that we struggle.

Why would Jesus tell us to choose our friends carefully? We can't mix two ways of thinking and hope they'll work together. Because our friendships matter to Jesus, we should know that He says, "I am the light of the world. If you follow me, you won't have to walk in darkness, because you will have the light that leads to life" (John 8:12).

Those who don't walk with Jesus walk in darkness. Christians walk in His light. Darkness either becomes light by following Jesus or it tries to make everything dark by doing everything it can to dim the light of Jesus in our lives.

As Christians we should shine our light, encourage those who carry the light, and welcome those who want to escape darkness. Following others into darkness for a long-term visit rarely helps anyone.

Jesus saves; we reflect His light.

Influences Matter. . . .

★ We act like the people we spend the most time with.

★ Jesus wants us to spend more time with Christians than those who don't follow Him.

★ We're influenced by the opinions of others.

- ★ Sometimes we worry too much about the approval of the wrong person.
- ★ If we really want to live for Jesus, there may be some people we can't hang out with.
- ★ A non-Christian doesn't live by God's commands and may like breaking God's law.
- ★ Jesus can use good friendships to help us when we need help.
- ★ We can't mix two ways of thinking and hope they'll work together.
- ★ Those who don't walk with Jesus walk in darkness. Christians walk in His light.
- ★ In friendships there will always be an influence to choose. We need to choose what kind of influence is helpful.
- ★ Make friends, but choose wisely.

If one person falls, the other can reach out and help.
But someone who falls alone is in real trouble.

ECCLESIASTES 4:10

CHAPTER 9
THE LIBERAL USE OF WORD GLUE

Jack and Mac were twins, identical in almost every way. They got their hair cut at the same place every month. They loved the same sports and played football together. They liked the same music, food, and movies. There was, however, one area where they were different. If Jack said he would do something, he'd get it done. If you asked Mac, you might get the same positive response, but he struggled to get around to whatever project he promised to do.

Jack passed his coursework with good grades. Although Mac was just as smart, he would simply forget to complete assignments. Trash was often left overflowing because Mac would get distracted and fail to take it out. Mac always had good intentions; he just didn't have a good supply of word glue.

Word glue is what it's like to take good intentions and actual promises and bind them together so promises are kept.

If you really can't do something, then you should just say no; but if you say yes and then fail to follow through, you don't help others see you as trustworthy, you may be thought of as deceptive or even lazy, and chances are pretty good they won't ask you again.

If your parents ask you to do something and you don't get it done, you can be considered disobedient. If you fail to complete assignments in school, your parents may be called in to have a conference about what can be done to motivate you to do your homework.

People who can't follow through on assignments have a hard time finding a job, and those who get jobs may lose them if they won't do what they are asked to do. Banks won't lend you money if you can't prove you can be trusted to repay. When your life choices suggest you have no interest in being committed, then this can even impact the potential for marriage.

Your parents have been given a job. They're supposed to help you learn how to be independent enough to one day live on your own. It sounds pretty easy, but when you refuse to cooperate, it makes things hard on your family, and they might impose new rules that make it harder on you. Let your word be your word. Make what you say and what you do match. Assume responsibility and prove you can handle it.

"If you are faithful in little things, you will be faithful in large ones. But if you are dishonest in little things, you won't be honest with greater responsibilities."
LUKE 16:10

Jesus wants us to use word glue, too. He wants us to be faithful or responsible in small things first. When we show that we can do what He asks, He may give us greater responsibilities. However, if we can't seem to do even the small things, then we probably won't find the opportunities for big things available to us.

If you're wondering if it's really that important to do what you say, think about what it would have been like if Jesus had said, "I will rescue people from their sin," and then changed His mind and apologized for not being faithful.

We're all glad that He did everything needed to rescue us, but Jesus wants us to see that *His* faithfulness needs to show up in *our* actions. If Jesus can save us from the punishment of sin, then we should be able to take out the garbage, clean our room, do our homework, and any other job we promise (or are asked) to do.

Jesus loves obedience. If you love Jesus, show it by the way you obey.

Our Word Matters. . . .

★ Good intentions and actual promises should always result in a finished job.

★ If you agree to do something, then do it.

★ When you fail to complete a project, you may be thought of as deceptive or even lazy, and chances are pretty good you won't be asked again.

★ If your parents ask you to do something and you don't get it done, you can be thought of as disobedient.

★ People who can't follow through on assignments have a hard time finding a job.

★ Your parents help you learn how to be independent enough to one day make your own living.

★ Make what you say and what you do match.

★ Assume responsibility and prove you can handle it.

★ Jesus wants us to be faithful or responsible in small things.

★ Jesus wants us to see that His faithfulness needs to show up in our actions.

★ If we love Jesus, let's show it by the way we obey.

Work willingly at whatever you do, as though you were working for the Lord rather than for people. Remember that the Lord will give you an inheritance as your reward, and that the Master you are serving is Christ.

COLOSSIANS 3:23–24

CHAPTER 10
THE WORK GETS DONE

Jeremiah couldn't wait to get to his grandparents' farm. They lived about an hour away just outside of the small town of Woodland Hills. Grandpa was old school. He didn't use a cell phone, didn't use the Internet, and rarely watched television. Jeremiah liked visiting because Grandpa had chickens, a big garden, and a small brook that ran through his property. Jeremiah could always do things at Grandpa's house that he couldn't in the city, and he planned on having as much fun as possible on this visit.

Jeremiah's smile drooped when Grandpa told him they were going to build a new chicken coop. No playing in the brook, no feeding the chickens, and no snacking on cherry tomatoes all day long. Jeremiah was at the age where he could help, and Grandpa needed help. Jeremiah took the hammer, hung his head, and walked slowly toward a pile of wood, rolls of chicken wire, and an old coffee can filled with nails.

Each of us is made to work with others. Sharing our skills is what makes businesses, families, and friendships successful. Each of us has something we can do well, and all of us have things we can learn from others.

A person standing alone can be attacked and defeated, but two can stand back-to-back and conquer. Three are even better.
ECCLESIASTES 4:12

The more people who help on any project means the project can get done faster and has a potential for greater success.

When Jesus came to put His rescue plan in action, there were times when He had jobs for His disciples. They had to gather fish and bread from a young boy to feed a few thousand people, they were told where to throw their nets to get the most fish, they had to look for a colt for Jesus to ride into Jerusalem, and they had to go fishing to pay taxes. Because Jesus is God's Son, He could have done all of this Himself, but Jesus was teaching a greater lesson. The disciples weren't supposed to think they were better than anyone else. They were supposed to work together to get the job done.

When religious leaders confronted Jesus about the good things He was doing, Jesus said, "My Father is always working, and so am I" (John 5:17).

By example, Jesus wants us to do our work to the best of our ability. He doesn't want us to stop before we're finished. He always wants us to be satisfied knowing that we do our best for Him. He is always pleased with our best efforts. This is true even when we get it wrong.

We don't want other people to give up in the middle of their work. If they did, we would live in a state of chaos. You couldn't ride in a car if someone hadn't been willing to stick to the task of building it. You couldn't read this book if many people had refused to diligently work to make sure it was completed. You couldn't live in a house if someone stopped building when the foundation was complete.

And I am certain that God, who began the good work within you, will continue his work until it is finally finished on the day when Christ Jesus returns.
PHILIPPIANS 1:6

Jesus is working on you. He never gives up on you. He never ignores you. He always longs for the best for you. Because you're alive, God is still working on you, and He has a plan.

Back on the farm, Jeremiah finished up the work on a new chicken coop with his grandpa. There were many things he wanted to do, but when Grandpa let the chickens loose inside the coop, Jeremiah saw what all his work had accomplished. Grandpa put his arm around Jeremiah and gave him a gentle hug. Jeremiah's help had meant a lot to Grandpa. The tools were put away, the woodpile was almost gone, and there was almost no chicken wire left. Every time Grandpa went to gather eggs or feed the chickens, he remembered Jeremiah, and Jeremiah remembered the hard work, the great conversations, and the fact that he never gave up. The work had been done—and it was good.

Diligence Matters. . . .

★ Each of us was made to work with others.

★ We all can learn from others.

★ Jesus had jobs for His disciples to do.

★ We're supposed to work together to get the job done.

★ If everyone gave up, we would live in chaos.

★ Jesus wants us to do our work to the best of our ability.

★ Jesus always wants us to be satisfied knowing that when we do our best, we're doing our best for Him.

★ Jesus is always pleased with your best effort.

★ Jesus is diligently working on you.

★ Jesus never gives up on you.

★ Jesus never ignores you. He always longs for the best for you.

Work at living in peace with everyone,
and work at living a holy life.

HEBREWS 12:14

CHAPTER 11
FAILING AT GOD'S JOB

Henry heard the weather report on the way to school. It said there would be cloudy skies and a chance for severe weather late in the day. Well, now he was home from school and the weather guy had been right about the cloudy skies—so maybe he was right about severe weather, too. He'd seen enough news reports to know that severe weather caused a lot of damage.

Lightning flashed as Henry watched. His stomach hurt. Would his world change because of a storm? He didn't talk to his family about his worry, but the thought of a "significant weather event" made it impossible for Henry to get much sleep. The thunder in the background and the wind blowing outside didn't help.

God has many jobs, but there's one we try to do for Him—worry.

Give all your worries and cares to God,
for he cares about you.
1 PETER 5:7

Worry is something God takes care of. Humans have never handled worry very well.

Every one of us has failed at God's job. He doesn't want us to worry, and yet we find some reason to place a death grip on fear. We worry about what people think, the weather, the future, the past, today, our friends, our homework, our pets, our family. . . You get the picture. We worry—a lot.

Jesus knew that we would make worry a priority. Maybe that's why He said in Matthew 6:27, "Can all your worries add a single moment to your life?"

Seriously. Think about it. How has worry helped you live longer? Most of the things we worry about never happen. Those that do would have happened whether we worried or not. Our sleepless nights, fear, and concern never positively change the outcome of *anything*.

Maybe we think that God isn't big enough to handle things so we need to help Him. We can't change the course of a storm, the heart of a friend, or what will happen in the future. God can, which is why He's perfect for the job of accepting your worry. Do you want to know how God handles your worry? He knows that because He's in control there is nothing to worry about. He takes your worry so you'll stop playing with it. He takes it for your good and not because He plans to worry.

Faith trusts that God will look out for our good. Worry's partner is fear. Maybe you didn't know it, but faith and fear can't work together. Faith has confidence that God is in control; fear believes there is no one who can help. Worries leave when you recognize God is in the room.

What do we do with all the time that's left when we give God our worry? Matthew 6:33–34 says, "Seek the Kingdom of God above all else, and live righteously, and he will give you everything you need. So don't worry about tomorrow, for tomorrow will bring its own worries. Today's trouble is enough for today."

The answer seems simple enough: seek God and stop worrying.

Henry woke up to sunshine and the sound of birds. Other than a few rain showers, there was no severe weather the night before. He felt a little foolish for being so worried, but this was a new day. Surely there was something new to worry about—or was there?

Maybe you're a bit like Henry. You tackle the world's problems by worrying about them. This job is like a truck without wheels. Sitting in it may give you something to do, but the view never changes.

If you really want to get rid of worry and you wonder how you're supposed to give it to God, Philippians 4:6–7 gives perfect instructions: "Don't worry about anything; instead, pray about everything. Tell God what you need, and thank him for all he has done. Then you will experience God's peace, which exceeds anything we can understand. His peace will guard your hearts and minds as you live in Christ Jesus."

We all want someone to guard and protect us, especially on the bad days. God can handle it, but when we try to take His job, we will fail miserably every time.

Trust Matters. . . .

★ God wants us to give Him everything we worry about.

★ Jesus knew that, left on our own, we would make worry a priority.

★ Most of the things we worry about never happen.

★ Sleepless nights, fear, and concern never change the outcome of anything.

★ God knows everything, which is why He's perfect for the job of accepting your worry.

★ Faith trusts that God will look out for our good.

★ Worry's partner is fear.

★ Faith and fear can't work together.

★ Faith has confidence that God is in control. Fear believes there is no one who can help us.

★ God takes worry for your good and not because He plans to worry.

★ Worry is like a truck without wheels. You can sit in it, but the view never changes.

★ When we try to take God's job of worrying, we will fail—every time.

"I am leaving you with a gift—peace of mind and heart. And the peace I give is a gift the world cannot give. So don't be troubled or afraid."

JOHN 14:27

CHAPTER 12
BAD DAY SURVIVAL GUIDE

Dylan was having one of *those* kinds of days. You know, the kind where everything that could go wrong. . .did. He couldn't find any clean socks because he'd forgotten to take them to the laundry room to be washed. The ones he wore were the least stiff and didn't smell as bad as the rest. Breakfast was cold by the time he got to the kitchen, and his little sister had given his toaster pastry a smiley face using pickles and squeezable ketchup. In his first class he discovered he'd studied the wrong history chapter, so instead of knowing more about the Revolutionary War, he knew more than he thought he should know about the Louisiana Purchase. If Dylan could reboot his day, he'd have done it much earlier—and maybe more than once.

What Dylan experienced isn't unique. We all have bad days. Some are worse than others, like finding out someone in your family is really sick or has been in an accident. Maybe you've lived through losing your house or not having enough food. Bad days come and bring us face-to-face with discouragement.

* *

"This is my command—be strong and courageous! Do not be afraid or discouraged. For the LORD your God is with you wherever you go."
JOSHUA 1:9

* *

God had a command. His people are to be known for their strength and bravery—not wimpiness and fear. God knows that each of us will be discouraged, but He's a big God who takes care of big problems. Trust God and stand strong.

Discouragement often shows up when people feel as if they face everything alone. They don't feel like they have anyone who can help them, or they feel like bad things only happen to them and no one else. They believe their struggles are much bigger than what other people face. They often want to give up.

Trust in the LORD with all your heart; do not depend on your own understanding. Seek his will in all you do, and he will show you which path to take.

PROVERBS 3:5–6

When you're discouraged, think of the Bible as a treasure map. There's an adventure for you within the pages. Encouragement, direction, and hope can be found in God's Word. The problem is that when people are discouraged, they may not spend much time in the Bible. They refuse to use the best solution to move past discouragement.

"Do not be afraid or discouraged, for the LORD will personally go ahead of you. He will be with you; he will neither fail you nor abandon you."

DEUTERONOMY 31:8

See, this bit of good news can change your perspective. Discouragement is put in its place when

we read God's Word. When you're discouraged,
you should read the Bible more than ever.

Do you want some more good news?

. . . .

God has said, "I will never fail you.
I will never abandon you."
HEBREWS 13:5

. . . .

Discouragement doesn't stand a chance against
God's best news, but the only way you will
remember what He said is to read it for yourself.

We can be discouraged when we don't get what
we want, receive news we don't like, or find out our
best efforts weren't enough for us to pass a test, get
on the team, or win someone's approval.

God wants us to know that we can rely on Him.
He needs us to know that He doesn't abandon
us or leave us. He always provides a way through
discouragement.

If you want to see if anybody ever felt
discouraged, read Psalms. If you ever want to see if
anybody found the other side of discouragement,

read Psalms. If you just want to think about something other than your own discouragement, read Psalms. This is a great book to read when you are discouraged. Don't be surprised if you end up praising God rather than hanging out with discouragement.

Here's a preview of coming attractions:

* *

Why am I discouraged? Why is my heart so sad? I will put my hope in God! I will praise him again— my Savior and my God!

PSALM 42:5-6

* *

Praise Matters. . . .

★ We all have bad days. Some are worse than others.

★ God knows that each of us will be discouraged.

★ God takes care of big problems. Trust God and stand strong.

★ Discouragement often shows up when people feel as if they face everything alone.

★ Good news can change your perspective.

★ When you're discouraged, think of the Bible as a treasure map.

★ Discouragement is put in its place when we read God's Word.

★ God needs us to know that He doesn't abandon us or leave us without a way through discouragement.

★ Psalms is a great book to read when you're discouraged.

★ Hope moves discouragement to a less important place.

This hope is a strong and trustworthy anchor for our souls. It leads us through the curtain into God's inner sanctuary.
HEBREWS 6:19

CHAPTER 13
BETTER DAYS AHEAD

Everyone in town knew Carter. He'd been in an accident that left him in a wheelchair. The accident was more than twenty years ago, but Carter wasn't bitter. In fact, he was one of the most joyful people around. He rolled through town offering a smile and kind word wherever he went. He told stories to children in the park, listened to stories told by older men and women at the nursing home, and laughed whenever someone told a memorable joke.

One day Carter was passing the school when Nate started his walk home. Nate was ending a bad day and just wanted it to be over. Carter started a conversation that lasted several blocks. By the time Nate got home, his attitude had changed completely. He waved to his new friend and hoped to see him again soon. Carter had given Nate the gift of encouragement. It was just the gift Nate needed.

So encourage each other and build each other up.

1 THESSALONIANS 5:11

Everyone needs encouragement. Carter loved to be encouraged, but he also knew God gave him the ability to encourage others. Those who know Carter are glad he shared that gift.

God encourages us through His words found in the Bible. We should encourage others in the same way God encourages us. Encouragement may look like one person trying to cheer another, but it could also look like someone offering hope, inspiration, or even motivation. These are all things that each of us needs.

If all we hear is, "You'll never be able to do that," or "Do you really think you're smart enough?" we can begin to believe we're not really worth much.

The words we speak and the words we hear leave marks on hearts. We can think the worst about ourselves without others saying "I told you so" when we're wrong. On the other hand, other people are not impressed when we try to prove we're better. Encouragement stops these poor responses from happening.

Carter understood something many of us struggle with. Even when *we* may need encouragement, we will always feel better when we think about *others* and offer kind words.

Did you know that God encourages us to do good things like encourage others? Second Thessalonians 3:13 says, "Dear brothers and sisters, never get tired of doing good." Whenever we think of others first, there is something that changes inside us. We pay less attention to our own troubles and discover a joy that can only be found when we pay attention to the needs of others.

Encouragement is refreshing.

*Good news from far away is
like cold water to the thirsty.*
Proverbs 25:25

Encouragement is something God builds into our lives.

We prove ourselves by our purity, our understanding, our patience, our kindness, by the Holy Spirit within us, and by our sincere love.
2 Corinthians 6:6

Encouragement is a language we're supposed to speak.

Let everything you say be good and helpful, so that your words will be an encouragement to those who hear them.
Ephesians 4:29

Encouragement should not be kept to ourselves.

If your gift is to encourage others, be encouraging.
Romans 12:8

Encouragement reminds us that as bad as things may seem right now, there are better days ahead. Encouragement says that the struggles we face right now will improve. The best encouragement reminds others of a faithful God.

Encouragement changed Carter. When the day is over and he's alone at home, he doesn't think so much about the fact that he can't walk. He's remembering his conversation with Nate, the stories he shared with children, and the stories he heard at the nursing home. Carter can also remember just a few years before when all he could think about was the struggles he faced. There was no time for others because Carter could only think about himself. Accepting God's challenge to encourage others had changed Carter's life.

Encouragement Matters. . . .

★ Everyone needs encouragement.

★ God encourages us through His words written in the Bible.

★ We should encourage others in the same way God encourages us.

★ The words we speak and the words we hear leave marks on hearts.

★ Whenever we think of others first, we pay less attention to our own troubles and discover a joy that can only be found when we pay attention to the needs of others.

★ Encouragement refreshes us and others.

★ Encouragement is something God builds into our lives.

★ Encouragement is a language we're supposed to speak.

★ Encouragement should not be kept to ourselves.

★ Encouragement reminds us that as bad as things may seem right now, there are better days ahead.

★ The best encouragement reminds others of a faithful God.

Encourage those who are timid. Take tender care of those who are weak. Be patient with everyone.

1 THESSALONIANS 5:14

CHAPTER 14
EMBRACING GOD'S BIG IDEA

Ayden handed another cookie to another child moving through the line. So many cookies—so many kids. Ayden felt stuck. He didn't enjoy this job, but it was his own fault. He was supposed to be at a meeting a week ago to sign up for a job at the Children's Fun Fair at church. He wanted to be the guy helping at the Dunk Tank, but he was signed up for the last job available. He passed out cookies to kids who didn't even seem grateful.

The children were seated, fed, and had finished their drinks when Ayden noticed a small boy sitting by himself at a nearby table. Something about the boy made Ayden stop to talk. He grabbed some juice and a couple of cookies and sat down beside the boy. "Are you hungry?" Ayden asked. This question was the start of something amazing.

*"And if you give even a cup of cold water to one of the
least of my followers, you will surely be rewarded."*

MATTHEW 10:42

God wants you to be generous. Giving money is
one way to do that, but there are many other ways
to show generosity.

Generosity comes from a choice to love.
It leaves selfishness behind. It thinks of the
needs others have before demanding more stuff.
Generosity helps, holds, and honors even when
there's not a lot to share.

*While Jesus was in the Temple, he watched the rich
people dropping their gifts in the collection box.
Then a poor widow came by and dropped in two
small coins. "I tell you the truth," Jesus said, "this
poor widow has given more than all the rest of them.
For they have given a tiny part of their surplus, but
she, poor as she is, has given everything she has."*

LUKE 21:1-4

These verses show why generosity has very little to do with how much money you have. Jesus was honoring the gift of a widow who had only given a couple of coins.

God's great idea of generosity has everything to do with what's going on in the heart and not how much is in your piggy bank. People come in all sizes and colors. Some have a lot—some don't. Jesus was telling poor, rich, and those in between that He wanted everyone who follows Him to be generous.

Some people give because they don't feel like they have a choice, while others are generous because they are willing to give back some of what God has given them.

We're generous because we learn to love the things God loves. We share because God shared with us. We shouldn't hold back when we see a way we can help.

Everything we receive from Jesus should overflow to other people. We receive love, forgiveness, time, attention, and mercy. God gives us what we need and sometimes more. All of us have something we can share.

Ayden discovered how true this was. The boy's name was Caleb. He had been invited to the Children's Fun Fair, but his friend hadn't shown up. Caleb didn't know anybody and had never been to Ayden's church before. Ayden immediately forgot how disappointed he was in passing out cookies. He became Caleb's big brother for the night. They visited the Dunk Tank, Duck Pluck, and Bowling for Bubble Gum booths. Ayden's generosity didn't cost him anything more than a little time, but Caleb is coming back to church each weekend—and he's bringing his family. Ayden's view on generosity changed, and God used his example to influence others.

Generosity Matters. . . .

- ★ God wants each of us to be generous.
- ★ Generosity comes from a choice to love. It leaves selfishness behind.
- ★ Generosity thinks of the needs others have before demanding more stuff.

- ★ Generosity helps, holds, and honors even when there's not a lot of resources to share.

- ★ God's great idea of generosity has everything to do with what's going on in the heart and not how much is in our piggy bank.

- ★ Jesus wanted poor, rich, and those in between to know that He wanted everyone who follows Him to be generous.

- ★ We become generous when we learn to love the things God loves.

- ★ We share because God shared with us.

- ★ We shouldn't hold back when we see a way we can help.

- ★ Generosity insists that everything we receive from Jesus should overflow to other people.

Teach those who are rich in this world not to be proud and not to trust in their money, which is so unreliable. Their trust should be in God, who richly gives us all we need for our enjoyment. Tell them to use their money to do good. They should be rich in good works and generous to those in need, always being ready to share with others. By doing this they will be storing up their treasure as a good foundation for the future so that they may experience true life.

1 TIMOTHY 6:17-19

CHAPTER 15
GUS FINDS HIS COURAGE

Gus explored the river bank while his friend Dex climbed a nearby tree. You never found one without the other after summer camp a couple of years back. That was the summer that Dex helped his new friend discover courage. Some say it was the obstacle course that helped, but Gus knew better.

So be strong and courageous, all you
who put your hope in the LORD!
PSALM 31:24

When you think of courage, you probably think of some daring acts of bravery that impress people and get your name in a newspaper or online blog. Courage can be found in small things done with a big heart.

Sometimes we're not courageous because we're afraid we won't be able to do what needs to be done. We think we can't do it because it's not our job. We can be afraid that if we try and fail, others will make fun of us.

Courage stays in the background when fear convinces us we don't know what we're doing.

Be on guard. Stand firm in the faith.
Be courageous. Be strong.
1 CORINTHIANS 16:13

Courage steps up when we understand that God walks with us. Courage grows when we realize we don't have to do this alone. Courage is discovered when we allow God to be strong through us.

I take pleasure in my weaknesses, and in the insults,
hardships, persecutions, and troubles that I suffer
for Christ. For when I am weak, then I am strong.
2 CORINTHIANS 12:10

Courage is a bit like faith. You don't know how powerful it is until you believe it actually has power. You will have fear until you decide to trust God and give courage a try. Faith comes when you trust a faithful God.

* *

This foolish plan of God is wiser than the wisest of human plans, and God's weakness is stronger than the greatest of human strength.

1 Corinthians 1:25

* *

Even when being courageous seems foolish, Jesus wants us to know that it matters enough to Him that we need to decide if we believe God is smarter and stronger than people. God's plans always give us opportunity to be courageous.

We have to be courageous to tell the truth. If we don't have courage, then we live with a message that can help others, but fear won't let us share it.

We have to be courageous to believe the unbelievable. Jesus loved us enough to be punished for our sin. His love offers forgiveness, a restored relationship with God, and a future home in heaven.

We have to have courage to follow Jesus—even when His plans don't make sense to others.

God chose things the world considers foolish in order to shame those who think they are wise. And he chose things that are powerless to shame those who are powerful.

1 CORINTHIANS 1:27

God knows that people think in a way that is different from the way He thinks. He understands it takes courage to believe what He says is true. He knows it is a brave person who believes truth can be found in His words. And when we have doubts, God still says, *"Be courageous."*

Gus never had any plans to try the obstacle course. He was fine watching from below. However, there was something that made him want to try. He just couldn't find the courage. That's when Dex introduced himself. A few minutes of conversation and a little encouragement gave Gus just enough courage to try the course. In the end, the course didn't change Gus; it was having a friend who walked with him that helped Gus find his courage.

Courage Matters. . . .

★ Sometimes we don't show up with courage because we're afraid we won't be able to do what needs to be done or that others will make fun of us.

★ Courage will always stay in the background when fear convinces us we don't know what we're doing.

★ Courage steps up when we understand that God walks with us.

★ Courage grows when we realize we don't have to do this alone. Courage is discovered when we realize that as we allow God to be strong through us then we are no longer weak.

★ Courage is a bit like faith. You don't know how powerful it is until you believe it has power.

- ★ Courage matters enough to Jesus that He asks us to decide if we believe other people are smarter or stronger than He is.

- ★ God's plans always give us opportunity to be courageous.

- ★ Courage helps us tell the truth, but fear won't let us share it.

- ★ We have to be courageous to follow Jesus.

- ★ When we have doubts, God still says, *"Be courageous."*

"Be strong and courageous! Do not be afraid or discouraged. For the LORD your God is with you wherever you go."
JOSHUA 1:9

CHAPTER 16
HOW DID YOU GET THAT?

Gil first saw the video featuring his baby sister, Maddy, in youth group. He saw it again in church and smiled. She was cute, but then again, she'd have to be—she was his sister. At two years of age she had been caught on video in the nursery. Someone asked her about her doll: "How did you get that?" She took a deep breath, looked at the camera, and said solemnly, "God gave it to me." They asked Maddy about her clothes, shoes, backpack, and sippy cup. Each time she answered, "God gave it to me." At the end of the video she smiled and said loudly, "Tank You, God!"

Gil knew that his mom had given Maddy the doll, clothes, shoes, backpack, and sippy cup. Still, her answer was cute, and it was just like Maddy to thank God. His entire family would remember Maddy's declaration for a long time.

*Whatever is good and perfect is a gift
coming down to us from God our Father.*
JAMES 1:17

Have you ever tried living without food and water?
It's not long before you decide this is a failed
experiment and you grab some food and something
to drink.

The same would be true for air. Hold your
breath for a few seconds and your lungs will remind
you this is a bad idea.

We can try to claim responsibility for the
clothes we wear, the house we live in, and the
vehicle our family owns. We can say that since we
used money we earned then we're responsible for
the food we eat, the grass we mow, and the furniture
we buy. We could, but we need to remember that
God gave us "ears to hear and eyes to see—both are
gifts from the LORD" (Proverbs 20:12).

Maddy had it right. We should thank God for
everything. We couldn't work without our body. We

couldn't eat without food. We can't drink without water. Everything we have can be linked to God. He made all the resources used to make new products. He created color, texture, and variety in all the foods we eat. He did all this before we ever showed a hint of gratitude.

- -

Give thanks to the LORD and proclaim his greatness.
Let the whole world know what he has done.
PSALM 105:1

- -

Even awards belong to God. Yes, we use our talents, but they're talents *He* gave us. That doesn't mean we don't celebrate and cheer for the person receiving an award, but we have to remember God made everything and everything works the way He designed it. We work hard because God gave us skills to share, so when we share those gifts we're honoring the God who gave them to us.

God has given each of you a gift from his great
variety of spiritual gifts. Use them well to serve
one another. Do you have the gift of speaking?
Then speak as though God himself were speaking
through you. Do you have the gift of helping others?
Do it with all the strength and energy that God
supplies. Then everything you do will bring
glory to God through Jesus Christ.

1 PETER 4:10-11

God's gifts should never be stored away for future
use. He wants us to use them *now* to help others. He
wants us to use our gifts to show honor to Him. We
can't do that if we want to take the credit. When we
give because He gave, then we're just doing what
we learned from God.

When Gil asked Maddy how she got an ice
cream cone, she was quick to say, "God gived it
to me." Gil was learning that Maddy was right.
When we give God credit for His good gifts, then
everything can be a reason to be grateful. Gil smiled
and offered up a quick prayer: "Thank You, God."

God's gifts start with life, lead to rescue, and

end up with Him in heaven. His gifts are always worth accepting—and sharing.

Giving Matters. . . .

★ We could claim responsibility for all we have, but God gives us everything we need.

★ Thank God for everything.

★ We couldn't work without the body God made.

★ We couldn't eat without food He created.

★ We can't drink without water He made.

★ God gave gifts before we ever showed a hint of gratitude.

★ We use talents that He gave us, so we should honor the God who gave them to us.

★ God's gifts should never be stored away for future use. God wants us to use them now to help others.

★ When we give because He gave, then we're just doing what we learned from God.

★ God wants us to use our gifts to show honor to Him.

"For this is how God loved the world: He gave his one and only Son, so that everyone who believes in him will not perish but have eternal life."

JOHN 3:16

CHAPTER 17
WELCOME TO THE GROWN-UP TABLE

Reid hated Christmas. Well, that's not technically true. He loved the stories. He loved the gifts. He loved the lights and songs. What he hated was Christmas dinner at Grandma's house. Well, that's not technically true, either. He loved the food. He loved to hear his grandma laugh. He loved dessert. What he hated was where he had to sit for Christmas dinner. Yes, that's what he hated.

For as long as he could remember he sat with younger cousins and his brother, Finn. They all sat around a card table with a bedsheet thrown over the top. Five people eating at a table that barely fit four was really uncomfortable. Brightly colored punch spilled whenever someone bumped one of the legs of the table, none of the chairs matched, and Finn kept telling the same jokes over and over again. *This* is why Reid hated Christmas.

When you're young, you want to be older,

and when you're old, you want to be younger. We all think there is something we're missing out on by being our own age. Young people want to be taken seriously while older people might want less responsibility. God wants us to serve Him at all ages.

Don't let anyone think less of you because you are young. Be an example to all believers in what you say, in the way you live, in your love, your faith, and your purity.
1 TIMOTHY 4:12

Sometimes people *think less of us* when we're young because we don't show any interest in being responsible. They think we can't be trusted with something big because we haven't shown we can take care of something small. Sometimes our actions prove them right. When you show you can be responsible, the way people think of you changes.

This is just as true for how you act as it is for how you choose to follow Jesus.

When I was a child, I spoke and thought and
reasoned as a child. But when I grew up,
I put away childish things.

1 CORINTHIANS 13:11

God wants us to have the wonder and awe of children, but in order to grow we have to learn more about Him. We will need to understand the difference between good choices and bad. We will need to do the right thing even when we don't feel like it. We will need training. We will need to approach God's grown-up table.

You're growing up. Jesus is willing to teach if you're willing to learn.

For someone who lives on milk is still an infant
and doesn't know how to do what is right.
Solid food is for those who are mature,
who through training have the skill to recognize
the difference between right and wrong.

HEBREWS 5:13–14

Sometimes we can think that spiritual food is only found at church. If this is what we believe, then we may be living on spiritual milk. It's tasty. It's nutritious. It's not enough.

As we learn more about Jesus, we should crave solid spiritual food. You can have full spiritual meals every day. Reading this is a great start, but you can always have more. God's Word is important, and it can help you "recognize the difference between right and wrong."

You can always share your meal, too. Other people need to hear what you're learning—even if they're eighty and you're much younger.

This Christmas, Reid once more sat at the card table waiting for the meal. Finn was already telling his joke, and the red punch was spilling over the sides of mismatched cups. He could see the adults sitting at the *big people's* table when a Christmas miracle took place. He heard his grandma laugh and say, "Reid, I think it's time you join us. I have a seat right next to me."

This was going to be a great Christmas.

Growing Up Matters. . . .

★ We all think there is something we're missing out on by being our own age.

★ Sometimes people think less of us when we're young because we don't show any interest in being responsible.

★ When you show you can be responsible, the way people think of you changes.

★ God wants us to have the wonder and awe of children.

★ In order to grow, we have to learn more about Jesus.

★ We need to understand the difference between good choices and bad.

★ We will need to do the right thing even when we don't feel like it.

★ You're growing up. Jesus is willing to teach if you're willing to learn.

★ God's Word is important. It can help you recognize the difference between right and wrong.

★ You can be an example to others who need to take their place at God's *grown-up table*.

We will speak the truth in love, growing in
every way more and more like Christ,
who is the head of his body, the church.

Ephesians 4:15

CHAPTER 18
ONE CHOICE CHANGES WHO YOU ARE

Tarrin knew his dad had made some bad decisions, but people always seemed willing to remind him. There was the alcohol, the bankrupt business, and time in jail. Kids don't let you forget stuff, even when they don't understand. Dad promised things would change this time. Tarrin had his doubts.

Tarrin's dad had been home for a couple of weeks, and Pastor Tim dropped by the house a few times to talk to the family. Pastor Tim talked about Jesus, and Tarrin's dad accepted God's rescue plan and said he wanted to follow Jesus. Tarrin struggled with believing his dad's decision was real—or would last. He'd tried to make better choices before and it hadn't worked. How would knowing Jesus stop the kids at school from talking about his family? How would it help others see his dad as trustworthy?

*The sinful nature wants to do evil, which is just the
opposite of what the Spirit wants. And the Spirit
gives us desires that are the opposite of what
the sinful nature desires. These two forces are
constantly fighting each other, so you are not
free to carry out your good intentions.*

GALATIANS 5:17

We all make bad choices from time to time. Those
choices always hurt us and often hurt others,
including those we love. When we struggle making
the right choice, there is only one truly great choice
to make—ask Jesus for help.

When you believe in Jesus, accept His rescue
plan, and read His Word to know His plan, your
identity changes. You are no longer a sinner with
no hope; you are a child of God who received grace,
forgiveness, and love. Before you choose Jesus, He
chose you. Talk about good news!

Following Jesus doesn't mean we'll never make
wrong choices. Sometimes it will seem we can't
help ourselves—we will make bad decisions.

I want to do what is good, but I don't. I don't
want to do what is wrong, but I do it anyway.

ROMANS 7:19

It can be a real struggle when we want to make
the right choice but fail. Jesus wants us to always
remember that when we accept His rescue plan,
He is the one we need to talk to when we need
help with making good decisions. The problem is,
we usually try to make the decision on our own—
without His help. That's usually when we mess
things up.

When we sin, Jesus doesn't look for ways
to make us feel bad. He wants us to admit we've
sinned and agree that we're wrong. That's when
Jesus can forgive us.

Don't you see how wonderfully kind, tolerant,
and patient God is with you? Does this mean
nothing to you? Can't you see that his kindness
is intended to turn you from your sin?

ROMANS 2:4

God demands payment for sin, and Jesus paid what we owe. His kindness should always cause us to want to turn away from *sin choices*. We are at our best when we show our love for Jesus by obeying His commands instead of thinking that forgiveness is our best first choice. If we do fail, we should always turn back to God.

Tarrin had seen his dad try harder, and when he failed he felt horrible, but that was before he chose to follow Jesus. Now there was something different about the way his dad handled mistakes. Tarrin was beginning to think something had actually changed in his dad. Tarrin finally had hope, and for reasons he didn't fully understand, he wanted to learn more about Jesus.

When you choose Jesus, it changes who you are. You become a child of God.

That's one amazing choice.

Choices Matter. . . .

★ When you struggle making the right choice, there is only one truly great choice left—ask Jesus for help.

★ When you believe in Jesus, accept His rescue plan, and read His Word to know His plan, your identity changes.

★ Following Jesus doesn't mean we will never make wrong choices.

★ Jesus wants us to always remember that when we accept His rescue plan, He is the one we need to talk to when we're trying to make good decisions.

★ Jesus wants us to admit that we've sinned and agree that we're wrong. That's when He can forgive us.

★ God demands payment for sin, and Jesus paid what we owe.

★ The kindness of Jesus should always cause us to want to turn away from sin choices.

★ We are at our best when we show our love for Jesus by obeying His commands.

★ We should turn back to God every time we make the wrong choice.

But God showed his great love for us by sending
Christ to die for us while we were still sinners.
And since we have been made right in God's
sight by the blood of Christ, he will certainly
save us from God's condemnation.
Romans 5:8-9

CHAPTER 19
NO SUBTRACTION ON MAPLE LANE

Mason was just waking up, but he recognized that smell—pancakes! He knew his mom had also purchased real maple syrup, which was a huge treat. Usually they had to live with store syrup that had no actual maple in it. That stuff had ingredients Mason couldn't pronounce. It made him wonder if they made it in a middle school biology lab.

Maple syrup? When it was real, you could taste the flavor, the sweetness, and it made you think you might just be visiting a snowy forest in Michigan to visit the very tree that offered the sap that made the world's most perfect syrup. No artificial ingredients, no substitutes, and no fillers. When Mason poured a four-lane highway of pure maple syrup through a stack of homemade pancakes, it was easy to imagine that this was going to be a perfect day.

For I want you to understand what really matters,
so that you may live pure and blameless
lives until the day of Christ's return.

PHILIPPIANS 1:10

The opposite of purity is impurity, but sometimes the opposite of purity looks like tolerating something God never wanted you to accept. An example? You're with friends and someone starts telling a joke that you know wouldn't please God. Will you substitute purity of thought for spending time listening to something that you know is wrong?

When you accept a substitute for purity, you always get sin. It's a simple mathematical equation. When you subtract purity and add cheating, it equals sin. When you subtract honesty and add lying, it equals sin. When you subtract forgiveness and add hatred, it equals sin. Purity means that any personal decision to subtract godly character and add a sinful choice should be avoided, and if we fail, then we will need God's forgiveness.

Purity is important for another reason. If Jesus hadn't been pure, then God could not have accepted His payment for your sin when Jesus died on the cross. Jesus never substituted anything in God's laws. If He had, He would not have been the perfect sacrifice for our sin. No wonder purity matters to Jesus.

If you keep yourself pure, you will be a special utensil for honorable use. Your life will be clean, and you will be ready for the Master to use you for every good work.

2 TIMOTHY 2:21

Purity is a choice that honors God and helps in our personal relationships, spiritual health, and physical condition. Purity pays attention to God's commands and doesn't try to figure out a way to avoid them. Purity is to our journey with Jesus what maple is to quality syrup. They go together perfectly.

Purity matters so much to Jesus that He sent

the Holy Spirit to help us make great decisions. No matter how tempted you are to sin, you should remember that any sin substitutions subtract the priority of purity.

Mason has tasted real maple syrup, and no substitute can compare. Psalm 34:8 says, "Taste and see that the LORD is good. Oh, the joys of those who take refuge in him!"

When you really believe God is trustworthy, that His Word is important, and that His plan should be followed, you will *taste*, you will *see*, and you will find *joy*. There is no substitute that will ever be able to take His place, improve His plan, or outlove God.

And when you can't get the math right and you fail miserably, you can ask God for new purity. Psalm 51:7 says, "Purify me from my sins, and I will be clean; wash me, and I will be whiter than snow."

Once you taste the goodness of God, you will begin to understand—nothing compares.

Purity Matters. . . .

★ The opposite of purity is impurity.

★ Sometimes the opposite of purity looks like tolerating something God never wanted you to accept.

★ When you accept a substitute for purity, you always get sin.

★ Purity means that any personal decision to subtract godly character and add a sinful choice should be avoided.

★ If Jesus hadn't been pure, then God could not have accepted His payment for your sin when Jesus died on the cross.

★ Jesus never substituted anything in God's laws. If He had, He would not have been the perfect sacrifice for our sin.

★ Purity is a choice that honors God and helps in our personal relationships, spiritual health, and physical condition.

★ Purity pays attention to God's commands and doesn't try to figure out a way to avoid them.

★ Purity matters so much to Jesus that He sent the Holy Spirit to help us in making great decisions.

★ No matter how tempted you are to sin, you should remember that any sin substitutions subtract the priority of purity.

Just think how much more the blood of Christ will purify our consciences from sinful deeds so that we can worship the living God. For by the power of the eternal Spirit, Christ offered himself to God as a perfect sacrifice for our sins.

HEBREWS 9:14

CHAPTER 20
INTEGRITY BOOT CAMP

Mr. Burke had been in the army. He was used to giving orders. He was used to having them obeyed. In his neighborhood, that meant no kid ever walked on his lawn, the newspaper was always hand delivered, and it was a brave thing to try to sell Mr. Burke anything. Few tried, few succeeded, and few would talk about it.

Cole was new to the neighborhood and hadn't heard about Mr. Burke. He was raising funds for a class project and bravely walked up the steps, rang the doorbell, and endured a glare that would wither grapes. In the end Cole left with a sale, but the purchased item had to be delivered by Thursday. If Cole was late, Mr. Burke wouldn't pay. Cole agreed.

"I always try to maintain a clear conscience before God and all people."
ACTS 24:16

If character is how you respond in difficult conditions, then integrity is found in the daily choices that God can use to build character. If deciding how to respond before you need to respond is critical to character, it is also important to improving your integrity.

People of integrity know what they believe, how they will respond, and do their best to keep their word. They are trustworthy, honest, and honorable. They make good leaders, good workers, and good friends.

They aren't superheroes, but they know Jesus, the greatest example of integrity, and they follow Him. Hebrews 4:15 says, "[Jesus] understands our weaknesses, for he faced all of the same testings we do, yet he did not sin."

Jesus understands what it's like to feel tired, frustrated, and angry. He saw bad behavior up close and personal, yet He did not sin. The integrity Jesus demonstrated is what integrity should look like in us. We should expect more from ourselves than we do from others. We should want to correct bad behaviors in ourselves, and when we work on ourselves, we spend less time pointing out the faults we see in others. We offer forgiveness even when we may believe it's undeserved.

Integrity may not sound like fun, but it is the best way to work with God in becoming people of good character. Integrity involves a blend of obedience and good habits. It shows up in the way we treat others and in how we respond to impossible situations.

* *

True godliness with contentment is itself great wealth. After all, we brought nothing with us when we came into the world, and we can't take anything with us when we leave it.
1 TIMOTHY 6:6–7

* *

We may be citizens of the nation in which we live, but as Christians we will be citizens of heaven forever. Jesus has given us what we need to live here, and He's preparing everything we will need in heaven. When we really believe this truth, we'll discover that we can be completely satisfied in what Jesus has given.

Cole had a delivery to make. He quietly approached Mr. Burke's door. He handed the ordered item to the man, who said, "It's Friday. You're late!" Cole knew it and calmly replied, "No charge, Mr. Burke. I'm sorry I couldn't get this to you yesterday. Maybe next time." Cole walked away having used money he had been saving to pay for Mr. Burke's item.

Maybe Cole's integrity meant something to Mr. Burke, but even if it didn't, it affected Cole. The shipment arrived late. There was nothing he could do about that. What he could do was honor his promise and not charge Mr. Burke. It was hard because Cole didn't have a lot of money, but it was a sign of growing integrity on the day when Cole did the hard thing in the right way at the right time.

Integrity Matters. . . .

★ If character is how you respond in difficult conditions, then integrity is found in the daily choices that God can use to build character.

★ People of integrity know what they believe, know how they will respond, and always do their best to keep their word.

★ People of integrity aren't superheroes, but they know Jesus, and they follow His example.

★ Jesus understands what it's like to feel tired, frustrated, and angry. He saw bad behavior up close and personal, and He did not sin.

★ The integrity Jesus demonstrated is what integrity should look like in us.

★ We should expect more from ourselves than we do from others.

★ Integrity involves a blend of obedience with good habits.

★ Integrity shows up in the way we treat others and in how we respond to impossible situations.

★ We may be citizens of the nation in which we live, but as Christians we will be citizens of heaven forever.

Jesus has given us what we need to live here, and He's preparing everything we will need in heaven.

- -

Choose a good reputation over great riches; being held in high esteem is better than silver or gold.

PROVERBS 22:1

- -

CHAPTER 21
THE HONORABLE TRUTH

Brody had a question for everything. As a child his parents were frustrated because every question was met with, "Why?" No matter how his parents responded, Brody's follow-up question was "Why?" It was a game that never ended, and no answer satisfied the boy.

That was a few years ago, and Brody doesn't always ask why these days, but the questions still show up: "If I do that, will you give more work to John?" Or, "Didn't I do that last week? Isn't that enough? How much are you paying?"

- -

Children, obey your parents because you belong to the Lord, for this is the right thing to do. "Honor your father and mother." This is the first commandment with a promise: If you honor your father and mother, "things will go well for you, and you will have a long life on the earth."

EPHESIANS 6:1-3

- -

The real simple answer to honoring your parents is because God said so.

If you're anything like Brody, you want answers. You want to know why God said to honor your parents. We just learned that honoring them is a command—not a suggestion. We learned that things will go well for us when we do. However, the greatest reason might be that if we can learn to obey and honor our parents, it will be much easier to obey and honor God.

"Anyone who wants to serve me must follow me, because my servants must be where I am. And the Father will honor anyone who serves me."
JOHN 12:26

Where should you learn respect, honor, trust, forgiveness, obedience, and love? At home with your family. Even when things aren't perfect, this is the first place you should experience these traits.

Some think their family members don't deserve respect and that God should allow them to skip obedience and honor. He doesn't. That may seem unfair, but unless you're asked to do something God says is wrong, then obedience and honor remain commands.

. . . .

"So if you sinful people know how to give good gifts to your children, how much more will your heavenly Father give good gifts to those who ask him."
MATTHEW 7:11

. . . .

You may be the only person in your family to follow Jesus. You may think this means you no longer need to follow your parents. Jesus says that even people who sin love and take care of their families. God can use your honor and respect to help your family see that Jesus really can make a difference. On the other hand, if you continue to show disrespect and refuse to honor them, then they may believe Jesus really doesn't do much to change anyone. This is *not* the message they should get when they see the way you respond.

There is a book in the Bible known as Romans.

The writer described some Christians who decided they didn't have to do everything God commanded. They wanted to pick and choose which commandments they liked. They acted worse than Brody. This is how they were described: "Their lives became full of every kind of wickedness, sin, greed, hate, envy, murder, quarreling, deception, malicious behavior, and gossip. They are backstabbers, haters of God, insolent, proud, and boastful. They invent new ways of sinning, and they disobey their parents. They refuse to understand, break their promises, are heartless, and have no mercy. They know God's justice requires that those who do these things deserve to die, yet they do them anyway. Worse yet, they encourage others to do them, too" (Romans 1:29–32).

These people found all kinds of ways to sin and then they encouraged others to do the same thing. That happens today when we find a command we don't want to follow, so we choose not to and then try to get others to do the same thing so we don't feel alone in our *sin choice*.

God's commands aren't suggestions, they don't

have loopholes, and they don't change just because
we think God was being too harsh. Learn to honor
God first by honoring and obeying your parents.
Then? Continue loving God with everything you've
got. Your parents will notice.

Honor Matters. . . .

★ We honor our parents because God said so.

★ Honor is a commandment with a promise.

★ The greatest reason to show honor is that if
we can learn to obey and honor our parents, it
will be much easier to obey and honor God.

★ We should learn respect, honor, trust,
forgiveness, obedience, and love at home.

★ Unless you are asked to do something God
says is wrong, then obeying and honoring
your parents remain important.

★ God can use your honor and respect to help
your family see that Jesus really can make a
difference.

★ When you show disrespect and refuse to
honor your parents, then they may believe
Jesus really doesn't do much to change
anyone.

- ★ God's commands aren't suggestions.
- ★ Learn to honor God by honoring and obeying your parents.

A wise child accepts a parent's discipline;
a mocker refuses to listen to correction.
PROVERBS 13:1

CHAPTER 22
HONOR IN THE FAMILY TREE

Declan and Sarah didn't get along. It was easy to call it a sibling rivalry. There were times Declan wanted to be nice, but Sarah didn't. When Sarah was interested, Declan wasn't. The brother and sister could go days without talking, or they could use their words to inflict wounds on each other. This cycle made life miserable for everyone in the house, especially Declan and Sarah.

Dad was frustrated and told them so. "One day when you're grown up, you're going to want to get along. Don't wait. Get along now." Neither was convinced this was a good idea, but at least they stopped complaining about each other until the next crisis.

Sometimes brothers and sisters can be meaner to each other than they ever would be to anyone else. Why is that? Maybe it's because home is supposed to be a place where you don't care what other people think. You express yourself without holding back. If someone is rude, there seems to be nothing to stop you from returning the gift, but you might send back more than you received.

Maybe you've heard people call other Christians "brothers" and "sisters." Sometimes Christians can have their own sibling rivalries. They may not look quite the same as at your house, but it happens. It's almost like God is saying, "One day you're going to want to get along. Don't wait. Get along now."

Don't use foul or abusive language. Let everything you say be good and helpful, so that your words will be an encouragement to those who hear them. . . . Get rid of all bitterness, rage, anger, harsh words, and slander, as well as all types of evil behavior. Instead, be kind to each other, tenderhearted, forgiving one another, just as God through Christ has forgiven you.

EPHESIANS 4:29, 31–32

These verses give us some great rules for dealing
with our families.

1. Watch what you say.
2. Give your words a positive purpose.
3. Encourage others.
4. No more hatred, anger, mean words, and
   gossip.
5. Watch what you do and how you do it.
6. Replace evil behavior with kindness and
   forgiveness.
7. If you need a reason to do this, remember
   God has forgiven you.

*Those who have been born into God's
family do not make a practice of sinning,
because God's life is in them.*
1 JOHN 3:9

No one has to teach us to do the wrong thing.
God tells us we were born with a heritage that
understands, identifies with, and practices sin. Bad
choices are nothing new for the human race. That's

why we need to be rescued from the penalty and punishment of sin. That's where Jesus comes in.

Making bad choices is easy. Romans 8:5 says, "Those who are dominated by the sinful nature think about sinful things, but those who are controlled by the Holy Spirit think about things that please the Spirit."

When you insist on doing the wrong thing, you're out of control. God pays attention to the way you respond to your family—at home and at church—and He can issue a warning sort of like the CHECK ENGINE light on a car. Once you've been warned, you may need some spiritual roadside assistance. If your responses aren't encouraging, kind, and forgiving, then perhaps it's time to ask God to take control because this isn't how God's children should treat each other.

* *

So letting your sinful nature control your mind leads to death. But letting the Spirit control your mind leads to life and peace.
ROMANS 8:6

* *

When our sinful nature is in control, we will do and say things that can seem humorous but hurt other people and can lead to an atmosphere that doesn't show respect. When the Holy Spirit controls our actions, we will know it by the peacefulness that follows every act of obedience.

Family Matters. . . .

★ Sometimes brothers and sisters can be meaner to each other than they ever would be to anyone else.

★ Watch what you say.

★ Give your words a positive purpose.

★ Encourage others.

★ No more hatred, anger, mean words, and gossip.

★ Watch what you do and how you do it.

★ Replace evil behavior with kindness and forgiveness.

★ God has forgiven you.

★ We were born with a heritage that understands, identifies with, and practices sin.

★ When you insist on doing the wrong thing, then you're out of control.

★ If your responses aren't encouraging, kind, and forgiving, then perhaps it's time to ask God to take control.

★ If we refuse to let God lead, He does have other ways of getting our attention.

As you endure this divine discipline, remember that God is treating you as his own children. Who ever heard of a child who is never disciplined by its father?
HEBREWS 12:7

CHAPTER 23
HUMILITY IN A "ME FIRST" WORLD

Bentley and Jake had been friends since before they could pronounce each other's name. Where Jake was tall and muscular, Bentley was short and skinny. The differences had never stopped the two from playing baseball together. They had come up through the ranks of T-ball, machine pitch, and now the first season in a new league where actual players would pitch. The two spent hours practicing. One would pitch while the other hit. One would throw while the other caught. The two were ready for the season to start.

The Bears posted their roster, and Jake was top of the list. Bentley's name was missing. The Lions and Tigers posted, and Bentley was still not chosen. Finally it was announced that they had found another coach and all the boys who hadn't been named to a team would play for the Wonder Boys. Bentley had found a team, but most who were honest considered the Wonder Boys a scrub team.

No one thought these boys could have made it on the other teams, and they wouldn't have played at all if they hadn't found a coach. Bentley wasn't the biggest guy on the team, but he'd probably played the most ball. That was, until the new player showed up.

The humble will see their God at work and be glad.
Let all who seek God's help be encouraged.
PSALM 69:32

There is a difference between being humiliated and being humble. When you're humiliated, you are made to look bad in front of others, but when you chose to be humble, you make an intentional choice to honor someone else by taking a step back and away from the spotlight.

John the Baptist did this when he saw that Jesus was starting His ministry on earth: "He must become greater and greater, and I must become less and less" (John 3:30). Before John said this, he was thought of as a great prophet and someone worth following. When Jesus arrived, John knew that his real place was in service to God's Son. He even encouraged his own followers to find Jesus and learn from Him.

People have always been used to promoting their strengths. Carnivals would be full of people with specials skills, and visitors would be called to come and see the unusual sideshows. Today we have social media along with video- and photo-sharing sites that promote our skills, interests, and abilities. God wants us to be careful about how caught up we are in being number one. Social media is very good at helping you promote. . .you. God's Book promotes the purpose for living.

* *

Let someone else praise you, not your own mouth—a stranger, not your own lips.
Proverbs 27:2

* *

Humility always says that others are more important and then does nothing to try to draw attention to oneself after making the statement.

When someone is lying about humility, he will say others are important and then find ways to demonstrate how valuable he is.

Truly humble people never claim to be humble—everybody just knows it. Those who claim to be humble rarely are.

Humble people are comfortable with who they are and don't need applause, awards, or honors to prove their worth. They do their best because they want to honor God. If other people notice, that's fine, but choices won't be made based on whether they get noticed. When you work in the shadows, it can actually be pretty comfortable.

The Wonder Boys were on the field practicing when the new player walked over to Bentley and said, "Hey Bent, wanna play catch?" Bentley recognized the voice and looked up. Jake had given up playing for the Bears. His best friend was now a Wonder Boy, and he'd rather play with him any day. Win or lose, they'd play each game together. To Bentley, Jake would always be a humble hero.

Who is the most humble person you know?

Humility Matters. . . .

★ There is a difference between being humiliated and being humble.

★ When you're humiliated, you are made to look bad in front of others.

★ When you choose to be humble, you make an intentional choice to honor someone else by taking a step back and away from the spotlight.

★ John the Baptist understood that he needed to step back as Jesus stepped up in ministry.

★ People have always been used to promoting their strengths.

★ God wants us to be careful about how caught up we are in being number one.

★ Those who claim to be humble rarely are.

★ If people are to notice what you do, let it be because someone else said something, not you.

★ Humble people are comfortable with who they are and don't need applause, awards, or honors to prove their worth.

★ God encourages those who work for Him.

Humble yourselves before the Lord,
and he will lift you up in honor.

JAMES 4:10

CHAPTER 24
BULLY IN THE HALL

Joel enjoyed most of his classes, the cafeteria food was fine, he remembered his locker combination, and his grades were pretty good. Still, Joel hated school. It wasn't because Levi called Joel names— because he never did. What Levi was good at was silent intimidation and threats. Joel understood the threats, and Levi had never been caught. This is why Joel hated school.

That was also before Joel became confused. There was a day when he saw Levi's dad drive up to drop him off for school. It looked like Levi was pleading for something. His dad had the same look of silent intimidation and threats Joel had seen on Levi. Suddenly Levi looked less like himself and more like Joel usually did. Maybe Levi had his own struggles.

The LORD is my light and my salvation—so why should I be afraid? The LORD is my fortress, protecting me from danger, so why should I tremble?
PSALM 27:1

In the Old Testament, David faced two bullies. The first was a giant named Goliath, and God helped David defeat him. The second was King Saul, and God helped David live through the bullying. These examples prove that not all bullies are kids.

It seems like every tactic bullies use was tried on David. Intimidation, threats, violence, lies, fear tactics, and turning others against him. Is it any wonder David would often cry out to God, "How long must I struggle with anguish in my soul, with sorrow in my heart every day? How long will my enemy have the upper hand?" (Psalm 13:2).

Bullies usually want control in one area because they don't feel they have any in a more important part of their life. For instance, when they don't have any control over choices and actions at home, they may force control over others at school or in their neighborhood. They may not really hate you; they may just want to prove to themselves that they can be in control.

If you were to compare the physical strength of a bully and those they intimidate, you may not find much difference. Bullies will try threats first. If the threats work, then they have found a victim. For bullying to work, they don't have to be stronger—you just have to accept their intimidation.

Jesus cared about bullies. He knew that many of them learned their behavior from someone who should have taught a different lesson. Jesus said, "You have heard the law that says, 'Love your neighbor' and hate your enemy. But I say, love your enemies! Pray for those who persecute you! In that way, you will be acting as true children of your Father in heaven" (Matthew 5:43–45).

Jesus had enemies. He faced bullies. He had religious and political leaders who tried to intimidate Him, and some plotted to kill Him. However, on the cross as He was dying to pay for our sin, He prayed, "Father, forgive them, for they don't know what they are doing" (Luke 23:34).

It may sound really strange, but if you show love to a bully and pray for him, you may find that you change the way you think about him, and he may change because your actions demonstrate something he's always wanted—someone who really cares about him.

There's always a reason why someone is a bully. Love has the potential of doing more good than detention, suspension, or even a public apology. You may not be able to control a bully, but you can control your response. Refuse fear and worry and hold tightly to love and prayer. We all want control. Sometimes the best control we have is how we respond to others.

Bullying can be frustrating and unnecessary, but God has shown in His Word that He can handle bullies, and His most effective method is a personal encounter with a loving response.

Responses Matter. . . .

★ Bullies may not really hate you; they may just want to prove to themselves that they can be in control.

★ Bullies don't have to be stronger—you just have to accept their intimidation for bullying to work.

★ When Jesus taught in Israel, He had enemies. He faced bullies. He cared about bullies.

★ When you show love to a bully and pray for him, you may find that you change in the way you think about him.

★ There's always a reason why someone is a bully.

★ Love has the potential of doing more than detention, suspension, or even a public apology.

★ You may not be able to control a bully, but you can control your response.

★ Refuse fear and worry and hold tightly to love and prayer.

★ We all want control. Sometimes the best control we have is how we respond to others.

★ God has shown in His Word that He can handle bullies, and His most effective method is a personal encounter with a loving response.

For God has not given us a spirit of fear and timidity, but of power, love, and self-discipline.
2 TIMOTHY 1:7

CHAPTER 25

ACKNOWLEDGING THE EXISTENCE OF EMOTION CONTROL

Zane seemed to live on a roller coaster. His emotions would often go down faster than they could go up. When he got a B in science, he acted like he'd single-handedly won a major sporting event. When he stepped in some food on the cafeteria floor, he acted like he just became aware of a plot to kidnap his dog. Zane could go from extreme happiness to anger in six seconds flat.

He was a lot of fun to be around in his good moments, but when he was angry or depressed, his friends struggled. They didn't know what to say or do to turn things around for Zane. Most of the time things just felt awkward.

* *

Better to be patient than powerful; better to have self-control than to conquer a city.

PROVERBS 16:32

* *

Emotions are a pretty wonderful thing. We love the feeling of accomplishing a goal, hanging out with good friends, and earning something we've wanted for a long time. On the other hand, you may hate the feeling of learning that your favorite pet has died, not placing in an event you trained hard for, or that something you've been planning for a long time won't actually happen.

Emotions are responses that show how human we are. It is a good thing to feel loved by your family. It is admirable to have a strong interest in the outcome of a sporting event at school. It can be overwhelmingly wonderful to be given a gift you really wanted. However, there are all kinds of emotions that we don't like and that others don't like to see in us.

For the world offers only a craving for physical pleasure, a craving for everything we see, and pride in our achievements and possessions. These are not from the Father, but are from this world.
1 JOHN 2:16

If emotional energy were money, then we spend way too much of it on the wrong things. We can get emotional about what we don't have, can't get, or never need.

Sometimes we use emotions to help determine how close we are to Jesus. If we feel warm inside about Him, then we think we're close. But Jesus had a different view. He says in Matthew 28:20, "Be sure of this: I am with you always, even to the end of the age."

What? No mention of emotion? Nope. Just a promise. He's always with us. He's close even when it doesn't feel like it.

We shouldn't use emotion to determine whether something is good or bad, either. That's why God gave us His Word. What He said in the Bible is truth. Using our feelings to change how we respond can lead to a wrong answer. Take reading the Bible, for instance. You can read for a while and then begin to feel like you're wasting your time, but your feelings don't line up with the truth in 2 Timothy 3:16: "All Scripture is inspired by God and is useful to teach us what is true and to make us realize what is wrong in our lives. It corrects us when we are wrong and teaches us to do what is right."

God has always wanted us to make wise choices, especially when our feelings don't agree with truth. We need to remember that God's plans are always more important than our emotions. God's best description of love in 1 Corinthians 13 demonstrates that love is a choice, not a feeling. Love is something we do, not something that can only exist if we feel like it.

God built each of us to experience emotions. Sometimes they are wonderful. Other times they can feel awful. God's truth always remains true no matter how we feel about it. Why? How we feel can change from one moment to the next, but 1 Peter 1:25 says, "The word of the Lord remains forever."

You can control your emotions by matching your choices with God's instructions.

Emotional Control Matters. . . .

★ Emotions are a pretty wonderful thing.

★ Emotions are responses that show how human we are.

★ If emotional energy were money, we spend way too much of it on the wrong things.

★ We get emotional about what we don't have, can't get, or never need.

★ We shouldn't use emotion to determine whether something is good or bad.

★ Using our feelings to change how we respond can lead to a wrong answer.

★ God's plans are always more important than our emotions.

★ God's truth always remains true no matter how we feel about it.

★ You can control your emotional reactions by matching your choices with God's instructions.

★ God has always wanted us to make wise choices, especially when our feelings don't agree with truth.

Imitate God, therefore, in everything you do,
because you are his dear children. Live a life
filled with love, following the example of Christ.
He loved us and offered himself as a sacrifice
for us, a pleasing aroma to God.

EPHESIANS 5:1-2

CHAPTER 26

WHEN MANNERS SURPRISE AND AMAZE

Sully hadn't lived in town very long. The kids all seemed to speak a different language. Sure, it was English, but some of the words seemed to mean something different, and other words that Sully was used to hearing never seemed to be spoken. Sully listened for words like *excuse me*, *thank you*, or even *please*. His parents expected to hear those words, and he tried hard to say them. His parents expected certain actions, and he tried to do them. They called these expectations *manners*, but Sully didn't see anyone else doing and saying what he was asked to do and say. Was it really so important after all?

* *

Sympathize with each other. Love each other as brothers and sisters. Be tenderhearted, and keep a humble attitude.

1 PETER 3:8

* *

Manners are God's top choice for right actions. Manners include attitude, encouragement, gratitude, honoring parents, kindness, gentleness, and honor. The list is much longer, but this is a great start in helping us understand manners.

Manners don't make fun of others, they don't hurt others, and they don't show dishonor.

One of the biggest reasons to use manners is to learn to be humble. Why? Having manners means to learn to put other people first.

Manners will hold open a door for a complete stranger, give up a good seat to visitors, and help clean up the house without being asked.

You may be wondering, *Sounds like manners means being nice to other people, but what's in it for me?*

Love each other with genuine affection,
and take delight in honoring each other.
ROMANS 12:10

What you gain from showing manners is knowing that you are pleasing God. You're learning to really love other people by choosing their needs over your needs. What's in it for you is a change of heart. Manners usually involve time and personal choice. Manners don't cost much more than that.

People with good manners are often remembered more than those who are rude, cranky, pushy, and ungrateful.

When manners are a part of who you are, you will show respect without being reminded. You will help others without being asked. You will demonstrate love when no one else pays attention. First John 4:19 says, "We love each other because he loved us first."

Like always, Jesus is a great example. He made the choice to love, and when He did, He showed us what manners look like. He was kind, patient, helpful, and put others first. He fed five thousand, healed the sick, and spent time with people no one else would talk to.

When we don't think we need to show manners the Bible tells us that manners show obedience to

God. Philippians 2:3 says, "Don't be selfish; don't try to impress others. Be humble, thinking of others as better than yourselves."

We don't need someone to show us a better way to be selfish. We've got that figured out. Manners show us the many ways God wants us to be selfless. Thinking more about others means we think less about ourselves. When we think less about ourselves, we will be less demanding, less bored, less irritated, and less rude.

Thinking of others means we will be more helpful, more encouraging, more loving, and more loved.

Sully didn't change the world by using good manners, but his choice was noticed in his new town and many used words like *thoughtful, kind,* and *decent* to describe him. Sully listened for words like *excuse me, thank you,* or even *please.* He wasn't sure, but he thought he was hearing them more than he used to. Maybe it always had been a great idea to show good manners. Today he was sure of it.

Manners Matter. . . .

★ Manners are God's top choice for right actions.

★ Manners don't make fun of others, they don't hurt others, and they don't show dishonor.

★ Manners will hold open a door for a complete stranger, give up a good seat to a visitor, and help clean up the house without being asked.

★ People who have good manners are often remembered more than those who are rude, cranky, pushy, and ungrateful.

★ When manners are a part of who you are, you will show respect without being reminded.

★ Jesus showed us what manners look like. He was kind, patient, helpful, and put others first.

★ The Bible tells us that manners show obedience to God.

★ We don't need someone to show us a better way to be selfish.

★ Manners show us the many ways God wants us to be selfless.

★ Thinking more about others means we think less about ourselves.

★ When we think less about ourselves, we will be less demanding, less bored, less irritated, and less rude.

★ Thinking of others means we will be more helpful, more encouraging, and more loving.

Most important of all, continue to show deep love for each other.

1 PETER 4:8

CHAPTER 27
THE HEART TO RUN

If there was one thing Tobiah knew, it was bicycles. He could fix, ride, and race with the best. Tobiah didn't play sports like basketball or football, but if you were to challenge him to a bike race, you'd see his competitive spirit rise to the occasion.

Tobiah saved to buy the best tires, top-of-the-line suspension, and road-glare sunglasses. He knew that a *biff* was a crash and *bacon* referred to a skinned knee. He was very aware that being *dialed in* was a good thing and *spring planting* hurt. Tobiah actually had two bikes. One for paved courses and the other for mountain trails. Some thought he went overboard on his bikes, but this was literally the course he had chosen, and he couldn't wait until his next challenge.

Don't you realize that in a race everyone runs, but only one person gets the prize? So run to win! All athletes are disciplined in their training. They do it to win a prize that will fade away, but we do it for an eternal prize. So I run with purpose in every step. I am not just shadowboxing. I discipline my body like an athlete, training it to do what it should.

1 CORINTHIANS 9:24–27

If you want to gain strength, you work out. If you want to learn, you study. If you want to follow Jesus, you'll invest time.

Let's look at some of the takeaways from the passage above.

1. A race is only a race if there are runners.
2. Racers compete to win.
3. Those who run require training.
4. Christians pursue their faith with purpose.
5. The best way to win the race is discipline.

Our *race of faith* is a race for one. Unlike a footrace, power walk, 5K, or bike race, the only person you compete against is yourself. You don't look at others and compare yourself to them. If you do, you'll think you're either better or worse and become prideful or depressed.

We should see other people who are also racing, but they aren't the competition—they are people who are traveling in the same direction. Encouraging others somehow improves our ability to run.

We don't grow in our faith simply because we have a Bible in our room, go to church on the weekend, or have friends who are Christians. We grow in our faith when we exercise our spiritual heart muscles. Psalm 7:10 says, "God is my shield, saving those whose hearts are true and right."

Our heart for God can become much stronger, or if left without discipline, it can become much weaker. Romans 2:15 says, "They demonstrate that God's law is written in their hearts, for their own conscience and thoughts either accuse them or tell them they are doing right."

Just because we invited Jesus to live with us

doesn't mean we will always make great choices. The truth is, we will continue to make bad choices when we refuse to be disciplined enough to read God's Word to discover the way He wants us to run the race. God didn't leave us without a plan, but part of discipleship is reading His race manual because He wants us to follow directions.

More than just His Word, God gave us something more—the Holy Spirit. This gift is like getting a spiritual GPS from God. When talking about the Holy Spirit, Jesus said, "When the Spirit of truth comes, he will guide you into all truth" (John 16:13).

Tobiah knew the terms used in racing a bicycle. Do we know the terms of the race of life—or do we just hope we're heading in the right direction without really knowing for sure?

We have God's Word, we have His Spirit, and we have a race. Let's learn to run.

Training Matters. . . .

★ If you want to follow Jesus, you will invest time.

★ The best way to win the race is discipline and training.

★ When you compare yourself to others who are also racing, you will think you are either better or worse and become prideful or depressed.

★ The other people who are also racing aren't the competition—they are people who are traveling in the same direction.

★ Encouraging others somehow enhances our ability to run.

★ We don't grow in our faith simply because we have a Bible in our room, go to church on the weekend, or have friends who are Christians.

★ We grow in our faith when we exercise our spiritual heart muscles.

★ Just because we invited Jesus to live with us doesn't mean we will always make great choices.

★ Part of the discipline needed is to read God's race manual because He wants us to follow directions.

★ More than just His Word, God gave us the Holy Spirit.

★ We have God's Word, we have His Spirit, and we have a race. Let's learn to run.

I press on to reach the end of the race and receive the heavenly prize for which God, through Christ Jesus, is calling us.

PHILIPPIANS 3:14

CHAPTER 28

HOLD ON: THIS COULD GET BRILLIANT

Henri's parents knew things would be hard for their son when they adopted him. He'd arrived from Haiti when he was four years old and spoke only Creole, the language of his country. When he went to school, things were harder for him because he was still learning English. Reading was hard because he always had questions about the meaning of the words he read.

Giving up would have been easy for Henri, but he remembered being in an orphanage in Haiti. Giving up in his home country often meant death. Henri worked very hard to learn. He studied every night and always asked questions. His parents were so proud when he brought his report cards home. His grades kept improving. Henri persevered.

*We can rejoice, too, when we run into problems
and trials, for we know that they help us develop
endurance. And endurance develops strength of
character, and character strengthens our confident
hope of salvation. And this hope will not lead to
disappointment. For we know how dearly God
loves us, because he has given us the Holy Spirit
to fill our hearts with his love.*

ROMANS 5:3–5

Perseverance climbs a mountain. Laziness is happy
with a postcard. Perseverance faces trials. Laziness
gives up at the first sign of work. Perseverance
believes better days are ahead. Laziness isn't sure
good days ever really existed. Perseverance offers
satisfaction. Laziness just doesn't care.

Perseverance is knowing what needs to be
accomplished and doing everything you can
to make sure it gets done. Sometimes people
will encourage you. Sometimes you will need
to persevere without anyone saying a word. By

holding on to the decision to endure, you will always do more than you think you can.

You can see perseverance in an athlete who continues to compete when injured, in a stage actor who forgets a line yet keeps in character, or in a student who pushes himself to learn when it may be more difficult than anyone realizes. Perseverance can be applied to any job you have to do.

Christians persevere when they pray, tell others about Jesus, and obey. These things may not come naturally to us, but prayer is the opportunity to talk to God, telling others about Jesus demonstrates how important He is to us, and obedience means we trust Jesus enough to follow His instructions. We persevere because Jesus told us to "take heart, because I have overcome the world" (John 16:33).

How can you grow up if you never face any difficulty? James 1:2–3 says, "When troubles of any kind come your way, consider it an opportunity for great joy. For you know that when your faith is tested, your endurance has a chance to grow."

The Bible tells us that there will be difficult times, but we need to endure. We need to persevere.

We should never give up. This may be hard, but it's an opportunity for great joy. Why? Because when we rely on God and really believe that He can get us through difficult times, we discover joy even when facing hard tasks. The finish line is closer with every step. Each step forward brings a sense that we are growing strong by never giving up. Each step brings security and trust in God.

Henri could have stopped trying. He could have thought all the work was just too hard. By enduring each struggle, Henri found a good life with his new family. His parents were proud of him, and through endurance Henri learned the value of finishing well.

Perseverance is God's brilliant idea because it gives us hope, strengthens our faith, and helps us cooperate with God's plan. Don't look at endurance as something that only looks like work. Endure because there's always something better at the end. Endure because God has promised to be with you. Hold on because God has a plan, and that plan is good.

Patient endurance is what you need now,
so that you will continue to do God's will.
Then you will receive all that he has promised.

HEBREWS 10:36

Perseverance Matters. . . .

★ Perseverance climbs a mountain. Laziness is happy with a postcard.

★ Perseverance faces trials. Laziness gives up at the first sign of work.

★ Perseverance believes better days are ahead. Laziness isn't sure good days ever really existed.

★ Perseverance is knowing what needs to be done and doing everything you can to make sure it gets done.

★ Trials develop endurance.

★ Perseverance is something God can use to help us experience joy.

★ Each step forward brings a sense that we are growing strong by never giving up.

- ★ Perseverance is God's brilliant idea because it gives us hope, strengthens our faith, and helps us cooperate with God's plan.

- ★ Each step we endure brings a sense that we are growing strong by never giving up.

- ★ Endure because there's always something better at the end.

Pursue righteousness and a godly life,
along with faith, love, perseverance, and gentleness.
1 TIMOTHY 6:11

CHAPTER 29
TRANSFORMED BY OBEDIENCE

Brice had an assignment. It wasn't a school assignment, which may be why he didn't pay as much attention to it as he should have. His youth leader at church had given him an envelope and told him to do the assignment inside before the youth group got back together again the next week. Brice put the envelope in his backpack and forgot about it.

Now the youth leader was collecting the envelopes when students came into the youth center. Brice grabbed his envelope, tore it open, and read, "Ask an adult to tell you why following directions is important. Write their answer here. Then have the adult hold this envelope, and take a picture of them. Send an e-mail of the picture and be prepared for some fun." Those that followed directions were invited to a special pizza and bowling night—all expenses paid.

Brice's response? "If I'd only known."

"Those who accept my commandments and obey them are the ones who love me. And because they love me, my Father will love them. And I will love them and reveal myself to each of them."

JOHN 14:21

A little boy starts to run into the street. His dad yells, "Stop!" The boy doesn't have time to ask questions—he either obeys or he doesn't. When the boy trusts his dad, he will stop. His obedience could be the difference between life and death as a car rushes by unaware that a little boy was in danger.

When we obey the commands of Jesus, we show that we trust and love Him. Obedience is a sign that we believe God knows more than we do. Obedience can be hard because we have to accept that we aren't in charge.

God wants us to learn to be obedient because if we don't learn this lesson, we can begin to believe we set the rules and no one can tell us what to do. Those who feel this way don't respect parents, teachers, or even those who help keep us safe.

*For the Lord's sake, submit to all human authority—
whether the king as head of state, or the officials he
has appointed. For the king has sent them to punish
those who do wrong and to honor those who do right.*

1 PETER 2:13–14

Obedience teaches us to be humble. When we don't
get to make every decision, we begin to learn that
not all decisions are ours to make. Obedience tells
God we have our ears open and are willing to listen
to His commands.

When we follow God's instructions, we learn
from Him by refusing to offer our own opinion.
Proverbs 3:5–6 says, "Trust in the LORD with all your
heart; do not depend on your own understanding.
Seek his will in all you do, and he will show you
which path to take."

God will trust you with greater responsibility
when you show you can follow the instructions He's
already given. Jesus said obedience is one way to
show we love Him. In John 14:15 Jesus says, "If you

love me, obey my commandments."

Obedience forms character, refuses pride, and demonstrates trust. There is always something better waiting on the other side of any act of obedience to God's plan. We may not always see it, but it could be to rescue us from the consequences of a bad choice, bless us for following God's plan, or prepare us for what God knows we're really good at.

Obedience doesn't save us; it just means we're willing to stay close to Jesus, the one who saves.

Obey and trust that God knows what's best. Obey and trust that God loves you enough to lead. Obey and trust that God's love can reach through you to someone in need.

Share each other's burdens,
and in this way obey the law of Christ.
GALATIANS 6:2

Obedience Matters. . . .

★ When we obey the commands of Jesus, we show that we trust and love Him.

★ Obedience is a sign that we believe God knows more than we do.

★ God wants us to learn to be obedient because if we don't, then we can begin to believe that we set the rules and no one can tell us what to do.

★ Obedience teaches us to be humble.

★ Obedience tells God we have our ears open and are willing to listen to His commands.

★ When we follow God's instructions, we learn from Him by refusing to offer our own opinion.

★ God will trust you with greater responsibility when you show you can obey what He's already told you to do.

★ Obedience forms character, refuses pride, and demonstrates trust.

★ There is always something better waiting on the other side of any act of obedience to God's plan.

★ Obey and trust that God knows what's best.

*"But anyone who hears my teaching
and doesn't obey it is foolish."*

MATTHEW 7:26

CHAPTER 30

THE FELLOWSHIP
OF THE REJECTED

The friendship between Hugh and Loki started in an unusual way. Some said they existed in survival mode. Their families wished things were different for the boys. They were the classic last-ones-picked for any athletic team. They loved technology and were considered "geeks" by others.

The two came from completely different backgrounds, but both had faced rejection, and from rejection a friendship was formed. Both knew how rejection felt, so they understood what the other went through. Having a friend was easier than going it alone.

* *

"If the world hates you,
remember that it hated me first."

JOHN 15:18

* *

We can be rejected because of what we believe, how we look, where we come from, the way we dress, and who we're friends with. Rejection often comes because we're not like everyone else. When people don't know how to respond to someone, they rarely make acceptance their first choice. Rejection can come for no reason at all. Rejection is often unfair, unwelcome, and unloving.

When we reject someone, other people may believe we think that person is unworthy. When we're rejected, others may think we're unworthy. Jesus thought otherwise.

"I am the gate. Those who come in through me will be saved. They will come and go freely and will find good pastures. The thief's purpose is to steal and kill and destroy. My purpose is to give them a rich and satisfying life. I am the good shepherd. The good shepherd sacrifices his life for the sheep."

JOHN 10:9–11

Because Jesus is the Good Shepherd, He knows our names, He shares our space, and He thinks enough of us to lay down His life so we could really live. We can reject God, but He doesn't reject us. If we really want to be separated from Him, He accepts our decision, but His rescue plan is always available. That's good news.

One of the worst things that happens when we're rejected is that we can become bitter. It's like our heart curls up, dries up, and gives up. All we can think about is the pain of rejection and the ways we will try to get back at the person who rejected us. Our actions can become worse than those who reject us.

Watch out that no poisonous root of bitterness grows up to trouble you, corrupting many.
HEBREWS 12:15

The way rejection often works is that after we hold tight to feelings of being unworthy, we can become bitter. When we're bitter, we welcome trouble. When we embrace trouble, our attitude infects others by inviting them to follow the same destructive pattern of thinking. It's hard to be happy around bitter people.

The sad part is, instead of changing our thinking and behavior, we blame poor choices on the ones who rejected us. The reason this is sad is because Jesus tells us repeatedly to forgive those who hurt us and be responsible for our own actions. If we remove the root of bitterness when we're rejected, we can escape the trouble that comes with letting it grow. If bitterness is a flower, it doesn't look good, the roots are deep, and it smells awful.

Those who hold tightly to bitterness might match the people described in Matthew 13:15: "For the hearts of these people are hardened, and their ears cannot hear, and they have closed their eyes— so their eyes cannot see, and their ears cannot hear, and their hearts cannot understand, and they cannot turn to me and let me heal them."

When we understand that we're accepted by Jesus, there's no room for bitterness, no time for hatred, and no place for revenge. Healing can take place, but we have to change how we look at things, whom we listen to, and how our mind reacts to God's instructions.

* *

I am writing to remind you, dear friends, that we should love one another. This is not a new commandment, but one we have had from the beginning.

2 JOHN 1:5

* *

Acceptance Matters. . . .

★ Rejection can come for no reason at all.

★ Rejection is unfair, unwelcome, and unloving.

★ Because Jesus is the Good Shepherd, He knows our names, He shares our space, and He thinks enough of us to lay down His life so we could really live.

★ We can reject God, but He doesn't reject us.

★ One of the worst things that happens when we're rejected is that we can become bitter.

★ If we remove the root of bitterness when we're rejected, we can escape the trouble that comes with letting it grow.

- ★ When we really understand that we are accepted by Jesus, there is no room for bitterness.

- ★ Jesus tells us repeatedly to forgive.

- ★ Those who are rejected often blame poor choices on the one who hurt them.

- ★ Rejection often comes because we're unwilling to be like everyone else.

Show others the goodness of God, for he called you out of the darkness into his wonderful light.

1 PETER 2:9

CHAPTER 31
YOU'RE NOT ALONE

When Mr. Maple asked Kael to head to the smart board, Kael wasn't prepared for the picture that popped up. "This is the *Daubentonia madagascariensis*," the teacher said. The class gasped and pointed at the size difference between the animal and Kael. The young man even stepped back after looking at the animal Mr. Maple said could be called aye-aye if *Daubentonia madagascariensis* was too hard to say. Most thought it was.

"Who do you think is bigger, Kael or the aye-aye?" Mr. Maple asked. Most thought the nearly hairless animal must be larger because it looked huge on the smart board.

Kael never needed to worry about the aye-aye. It was part of the lemur family, ate bugs, and wasn't much bigger than a rodent. It just looked scary—just like the struggles we face every day. Each of us will face difficulties that seem bigger than they really are.

*The LORD is my light and my salvation—so why
should I be afraid? The LORD is my fortress,
protecting me from danger, so why should I tremble?*
PSALM 27:1

We all face struggles we don't understand. Psalm
23 is God's road map through the things that cause
a battle between trust and fear. When we take the
time to learn what it says, it can change the way we
view every struggle we will face.

The LORD is my shepherd; I have all that I need.
PSALM 23:1

The Shepherd is God, and when He leads, it's
always enough.

He lets me rest in green meadows; he leads me beside
peaceful streams. He renews my strength. He guides
me along right paths, bringing honor to his name.
PSALM 23:2–3

The Shepherd always takes care of us and gives us
strength. He has a plan He wants us to follow, and
there will never be a question about who helped us
through hard times.

Even when I walk through the darkest valley, I will
not be afraid, for you are close beside me. Your
rod and your staff protect and comfort me.
PSALM 23:4

We *will* go through dark struggles. When we do,
God always walks with us, protecting us from harm
and comforting us when we fear the unknown. We
have no reason to be afraid.

*You prepare a feast for me in the presence of
my enemies. You honor me by anointing my
head with oil. My cup overflows with blessings.*
PSALM 23:5

Even when we struggle, we should remember God
is for us, takes care of us, and meets our needs.
When we remember the many ways God has
blessed us, we can become overwhelmed by how
much God loves us.

*Surely your goodness and unfailing love
will pursue me all the days of my life,
and I will live in the house of the LORD forever.*
PSALM 23:6

Once we understand how much God loves and takes
care of us, we can accept the fact that no matter how
many struggles we face, God's love never leaves, His
mercy is always available, and we never have to be

separated from all the gifts God has to offer.

Struggles offer opportunities to grow, a choice to trust, and a chance to follow God's great plan. When we face struggles, we can feel that no one understands, no one will help, and no one cares. Psalm 23 helps us see that God never leaves us even if others walk away.

"For the LORD your God is living among you. He is a mighty savior. He will take delight in you with gladness. With his love, he will calm all your fears. He will rejoice over you with joyful songs."

ZEPHANIAH 3:17

Struggles Matter. . . .

★ Struggles cause a battle between trust and fear.

★ God always takes care of us and gives us strength.

★ When we go through struggles, God always walks with us, protecting us from harm and comforting us when we fear the unknown.

- ★ God is for us, takes care of us, and meets our needs.

- ★ When we remember the many ways God has blessed us, we can become overwhelmed by how much He loves us.

- ★ Once we understand how much God loves us, we never have to be separated from all the gifts He has to offer.

- ★ Struggles offer opportunities to grow, a choice to trust, and a chance to follow God's great plan.

- ★ When we face struggles, we can feel that no one understands, no one is willing to help, and no one cares.

- ★ Psalm 23 helps us see that God never leaves us even if others walk away.

"For I know the plans I have for you," says the LORD. "They are plans for good and not for disaster, to give you a future and a hope."

JEREMIAH 29:11

CHAPTER 32
GOD TIME—ANY TIME

Dad was proud of Gaige. He had accepted the rescue plan of Jesus and wanted to know more about Him. He wanted to read something epic, so Dad suggested Exodus. He wanted to know more about how to talk to God, and Dad pointed him to Psalms. He wanted to know more about Jesus, so Dad showed him the book of John.

In between schoolwork, chores, and friends, Gaige read, and as he read he discovered more about God. Learning more about God helped Gaige see Him as absolutely amazing. He was actually having a conversation with God. Gaige would say what he needed to say when he prayed, and God would say what He needed to say in the Bible. A clear message was coming through.

I have hidden your word in my heart,
that I might not sin against you. I praise you,
O LORD; teach me your decrees.

PSALM 119:11-12

God's Word is always available for us to read. We can read a printed Bible, we can read His Word online, and we can even read on a cell phone. The Bible may seem too hard to understand, but not if you spend time learning from the God who rescued you.

God loves you and never hides His plans from you. When we feel lost, it's probably because we haven't been reading His Word. Becoming a Christian and never reading God's Word is like knowing you have a test in school but never studying. You may have some idea about the topic of the test, but you don't know the specifics because you haven't read them.

There is a group of verses that should be the opening training course for why we read God's Word. See if this helps.

The instructions of the Lord are perfect,
reviving the soul. The decrees of the Lord
are trustworthy, making wise the simple.
PSALM 19:7

Reading God's instructions refreshes us. God's laws can be trusted to make us wise.

The commandments of the LORD are right,
bringing joy to the heart. The commands of
the LORD are clear, giving insight for living.
PSALM 19:8

We experience joy when our actions match God's instructions. When we follow God, He will always make sure we know how to live.

Reverence for the LORD is pure, lasting forever.
The laws of the LORD are true; each one is fair.
PSALM 19:9

God should be honored, and it's always the right choice. God's laws are fair and should be followed.

They are more desirable than gold, even the finest gold. They are sweeter than honey, even honey dripping from the comb.

PSALM 19:10

God's words are worth more than gold and are sweeter than honey. Our greatest treasure should be knowing God.

They are a warning to your servant, a great reward for those who obey them.

PSALM 19:11

Reading God's Word can warn us of dangers to avoid. Spending time with God helps us learn what He wants so we can obey His commands. There is a great reward for those who seek, follow, and obey. It starts with reading God's Word.

When Jesus was tempted, He replied by quoting God's Word. When He faced challenges,

Jesus prayed. When He taught His disciples, He shared verses they would recognize so they would understand what He was saying. Jesus gives us a great example of how and why we include prayer and Bible study in our everyday lives—it puts us in touch with God, it dials us in to what He wants, and it helps us identify our purpose in *His* plan.

If Gaige's dad was excited to see his son reading the Bible and praying, imagine how our willingness to talk to Him pleases God.

Devote yourselves to prayer with an
alert mind and a thankful heart.

COLOSSIANS 4:2

Communicating with God Matters. . . .

★ God loves you and never hides His plans from you.

★ When we feel lost, it's probably because we haven't been reading God's Word.

★ God's laws can be trusted to make us wise.

- ★ We experience joy when our actions match God's instructions.

- ★ God's laws are fair and should be followed.

- ★ God's Word is worth more than gold.

- ★ Reading God's Word can warn us of dangers to avoid.

- ★ Spending time with God helps us learn what He wants so we can obey His commands.

- ★ When Jesus was tempted, He replied by quoting God's Word.

- ★ When He faced challenges, Jesus prayed.

- ★ When He taught His disciples, Jesus shared verses they would recognize so they would understand what He was saying.

- ★ Prayer and Bible study puts us in touch with God, it dials us in to what He wants, and it helps us identify our purpose in *His* plan.

For the word of God is alive and powerful. It is sharper than the sharpest two-edged sword, cutting between soul and spirit, between joint and marrow. It exposes our innermost thoughts and desires.

HEBREWS 4:12

CHAPTER 33
A TIME TO TURN AROUND

Poor choices were not uncommon for Ross. His family didn't go to church and rarely talked of God in a respectful way. No one led, so there was no one to follow. That's why Ross found it strange that he had said yes to his friend Quinten's offer to go to church. "No," Quinten had said, "you don't have to wear anything special." So Ross found himself in a chair, in a church, in a state of anxiety.

"Repentance," said the speaker, "isn't just saying you're sorry. It's regretting bad decisions enough to turn around and go a new way. Repentance agrees that the way you've been doing things isn't working and the only real choice is to change direction. God will accept you right where you are and lead you in a new direction with better choices, encouraging friends, and all the forgiveness you'll ever need. Repentance never leaves you like it found you." There was more, but Ross was left to think about what living life a new way looked like.

*Prove by the way you live that you have
repented of your sins and turned to God.*

MATTHEW 3:8

You've probably heard that grace covers sin. This is because Jesus paid the price for our sin debt. Grace is God's loving response to those who accept His rescue plan.

Repentance is our best response when we are first introduced to grace. When we see what Jesus gave up in order to save us, we have a choice. We can continue doing everything exactly as we've always done it, or we turn away from those choices and follow a new leader.

*For the kind of sorrow God wants us to experience
leads us away from sin and results in salvation.
There's no regret for that kind of sorrow.
But worldly sorrow, which lacks repentance,
results in spiritual death.*

2 CORINTHIANS 7:10

We should be sad when we make wrong choices. God wants that sadness to move us away from sin and toward Him.

Repentance doesn't make us perfect. We'll have to turn away from poor choices our entire life. The problem we'll face is becoming so comfortable with poor choices that we stop coming back to God. We might think that God has an exception for us or maybe He doesn't care as much as He used to. We can actually convince ourselves that we're doing pretty good.

The need to repent was a message Jesus focused on a lot. In Luke 5:32 Jesus said, "I have come to call not those who think they are righteous, but those who know they are sinners and need to repent."

Jesus is the only one who can remove the penalty for sin, the only one who can offer new life, and the only one who loves you enough to forgive you every time you ask.

Repentance is our choice. It recognizes what's really hidden in our heart, believes Jesus offers a better life, and accepts grace where punishment had been expected.

Many of our choices offend a perfect God. The penalty for breaking God's law has never changed—death. The incredible rescue plan that accepted the sacrificial death of Jesus on the cross paid that penalty price. We can be forgiven. We can be rescued. We can become children of God. Our decision is to believe that Jesus was the only one able to rescue us, and then to repent or turn away from those things that have kept us from God.

This is why we can come to God just as we are, but He never wants us to stay where we were. He has plans for you that can't happen if you won't turn in His direction.

Repentance Matters. . . .

★ Repentance never leaves you like it found you.

★ Grace is God's loving response to those who accept His rescue plan.

★ Repentance is our best response when we are first introduced to grace.

★ God wants us to be sad when we make wrong choices. He wants that sadness to move us away from sin and toward Him.

- ★ We will have to turn away from poor choices our entire life.

- ★ Jesus is the only one who can remove the penalty for sin, the only one who can offer new life, and the only one who loves you enough to forgive you every time you ask.

- ★ Repentance recognizes what's really hidden in our heart, believes Jesus offers a better life, and accepts grace where it had only expected punishment.

- ★ Many of our choices offend a perfect God.

- ★ Jesus was the only one able to rescue us.

- ★ God has plans for you that can't happen if you won't turn in His direction.

* *

The Lord isn't really being slow about his promise, as some people think. No, he is being patient for your sake. He does not want anyone to be destroyed, but wants everyone to repent.

2 PETER 3:9

* *

CHAPTER 34

THE SEEKING-FINDING-LEARNING-FOLLOWING PRINCIPLE

It's a few months since Ross changed directions and started following Jesus. It's been hard because his family didn't understand or even encourage his decision. He had changed, and that made them uncomfortable.

Ross had learned the "Seeking-Finding-Learning-Following" principle, and he was putting it into practice. In Jeremiah 29:13 God says, "If you look for me wholeheartedly, you will find me." This is where Ross started. The principle looks like this: Seek God—*find* Him. Find God—*learn* from Him. Learn from God—*follow* what He says. Ross was praying his family would join him someday.

"His purpose was for the nations to seek after God and perhaps feel their way toward him and find him—though he is not far from any one of us."

ACTS 17:27

Seeking

All treasure hunters want proof that a treasure exists. They don't spend time looking for something that lives in their imagination. They will study maps, journals, and stories of the treasure's location. It's only when they believe in the existence of the treasure that they begin to seek. If no one seeks, the process ends too soon.

God wants us to be treasure seekers. The difference is, He wants us to seek treasure in our relationship with Him. If we seek Him, we will find Him.

The LORD looks down from heaven on the entire human race; he looks to see if anyone is truly wise, if anyone seeks God.

PSALM 14:2

Finding

God wants to be found. Deep down we want to be found by God. He never plays hide-and-seek.

*Anyone who wants to come to him must
believe that God exists and that he
rewards those who sincerely seek him.*

HEBREWS 11:6

You'll also discover that "everyone who seeks, finds" (Matthew 7:8).

Learning

People don't become doctors, lawyers, or teachers without learning. They attend school, complete assignments, take tests, and demonstrate they know the material before they're allowed to actually do what they were taught. This is a form of learning that should make sense to Christians. God wants us to attend His school, complete assignments, endure tests of faith, and demonstrate that we understand what He's been teaching. This is called discipleship, and it's an important concept if we're going to understand how to do what God asks us to do.

As I learn your righteous regulations,
I will thank you by living as I should!
PSALM 119:7

Following

This step will last the rest of your life. If you're learning what God says, then the next step is to follow His instructions. You don't just know what He says; you have to do what He asks. This means you can't sit on the sidelines watching other people follow. You have to move in the direction He leads. You can't ask for status updates from God while you sit on the couch. You can't look in your inbox hoping for just enough news from God to get you by. You need to read what He says and do what He asks.

But don't just listen to God's word. You must do what it says. Otherwise, you are only fooling yourselves.
JAMES 1:22

You can't start to follow without knowing who you follow, you can't find if you never seek, and you can't learn something when you refuse to study.

God is worthy to be followed, has many things to teach, and asks us to walk with Him.

Not everyone is at the same place at the same time. Some are seeking while others are following. Some are finding while others are learning. None of us will be perfect in how we do that. This may be why God wants each of us to "make allowance for each other's faults, and forgive anyone who offends you. Remember, the Lord forgave you, so you must forgive others" (Colossians 3:13).

Ross is learning and following. His family is just beginning to seek. Ross is praying they find Jesus. His friends are, too.

Seeking, Finding, Learning, and Following Matters. . . .

★ Seek God—find Him. Find God—learn from Him. Learn from God—follow what He says.

★ God wants us to seek treasure in our relationship with Him.

★ God wants to be found. He never plays hide-and-seek.

★ God wants us to attend His school, complete assignments, endure tests of faith, and demonstrate that we understand what He's been teaching.

★ Discipleship is important if we're going to understand how to do what God asks us to do.

★ If you are learning what God says, then the next step is to follow His instructions.

★ We need to read what God says and do what He asks.

★ You can't start to follow without knowing who you follow, you can't find if you never seek, and you can't learn something when you refuse to study.

★ God is worthy to be followed, has many things to teach, and asks us to walk with Him.

"Therefore, go and make disciples."
MATTHEW 28:19

CHAPTER 35
THE NEGLECTED LIST OF WANTS

Cayson had watched his mom toss spare change in a jar for months. She told him it was for something special but would never tell him what. He saw her looking at watches when they went to the store. She would sigh, smile at the clerk, and they would walk away again. Cayson was certain he knew what was *special* to his mom, and he was excited to see her get the watch.

When Cayson arrived home from school one day, his mom asked him to come sit beside her. She smiled and told him that the special gift had arrived. Cayson looked for a watch on her arm, but she only held an envelope in her hand. The envelope contained a permission slip for him to go on a school trip he never thought they could afford, which is why he'd never asked to go. The spare change had been for his needs. The watch would wait.

Don't look out only for your own interests,
but take an interest in others, too.
PHILIPPIANS 2:4

Self-denial is the term used to describe taking an interest in others before marking an item off our own wish list. It's a skill many parents have. What they think they want can always wait when they know there is a need or special opportunity for their children.

Self-denial lets others choose first, refuses a personal purchase, and considers other opinions and needs before one's own.

God knew it would be hard for us to give up our own plans, desires, and wants in order to help someone else. Perhaps He did this so we could understand what parents do for us. Sometimes we give up something we want because it may be the only way someone else can have something he or she really needs.

Dear children, let's not merely say that we love each other; let us show the truth by our actions.

1 JOHN 3:18

Love is never just words. When we say we love others, it will only be believed when they see that we mean it by our actions. We might say it's sad that people have needs, but then we do nothing to help.

Suppose you see a brother or sister who has no food or clothing, and you say, "Good-bye and have a good day; stay warm and eat well"—but then you don't give that person any food or clothing. What good does that do?

JAMES 2:15–16

The opposite of self-denial is selfishness. You can see this in people who demand their own way, insist on a very specific gift, and refuse to consider the needs of others. They may believe they are too

214

important, powerful, or respected to do anything that looks like serving others.

Don't be selfish; don't try to impress others.
Be humble, thinking of others as better than yourselves.

PHILIPPIANS 2:3

Jesus demonstrated self-denial. He's the Son of God, but He came to serve us by putting together the most impressive rescue plan ever known to man. He lived among us, shared our sorrows, and died in our place. He could have demanded something better, but He humbled Himself and taught us by example to do the same.

You must have the same attitude that Christ Jesus had. Though he was God, he did not think of equality with God as something to cling to. Instead, he gave up his divine privileges; he took the humble position of a slave and was born as a human being.

PHILIPPIANS 2:5–7

Cayson saw how long Mom had worked to pay for his trip, so he quietly saved his own money over a few months to pay for the new watch his mom had been wanting. Her tears kind of embarrassed him, but it also helped him see the benefit of putting the interests of others ahead of his own. It felt pretty wonderful.

Self-Denial Matters. . . .

★ *Self-denial* is the term used to describe taking an interest in others before marking an item off our own wish list.

★ Self-denial lets others choose first.

★ Self-denial considers others' needs before one's own.

★ God knew that it would be hard for us to give up our own plans, desires, and wants in order to help someone else.

★ Sometimes we must give up something we want because it may be the only way someone else can have something he or she really needs.

★ When we say we love others, it will only be believed when they see that we mean it by our actions.

★ The opposite of self-denial is selfishness.

★ Jesus came to serve us by putting together the most impressive rescue plan ever known to man.

★ Jesus humbled Himself and taught us by example to do the same.

Is there any encouragement from belonging to Christ? Any comfort from his love? Any fellowship together in the Spirit? Are your hearts tender and compassionate? Then make me truly happy by agreeing wholeheartedly with each other, loving one another, and working together with one mind and purpose.

PHILIPPIANS 2:1–2

CHAPTER 36
WHATCHA THINKIN'?

Bridger had trouble thinking. It's not that he couldn't think; it's that his brain kept moving from one thought to the next, never leaving him time to concentrate. Bridger also struggled with some thoughts he didn't want to think. Sometimes the only thoughts that would stay longer than the others were thoughts he'd be ashamed to talk about with anyone.

It wasn't long before Bridger didn't want to talk to anyone because he didn't want to say something that might result in questions he didn't want to answer about the thoughts he didn't want to have.

So prepare your minds for action and exercise self-control. Put all your hope in the gracious salvation that will come to you when Jesus Christ is revealed to the world.

1 PETER 1:13

Did you know the Bible can be a great tool to help you bring your thoughts into focus? By concentrating on what God says, we can tame the thoughts that want to run a marathon through our brain.

The things we allow our mind to spend the most time with are the things that will fill our heart. There is a connection between what we think and how our heart responds.

"A good person produces good things from the treasury of a good heart, and an evil person produces evil things from the treasury of an evil heart. What you say flows from what is in your heart."
LUKE 6:45

Our heart and mind work together to either follow God or a new path that seems entertaining. God wants us to ask Him for help—and then accept it. That may sound like a strange statement, but sometimes we ask for His wisdom, but we don't really want it.

If you need wisdom, ask our generous God, and he will give it to you. He will not rebuke you for asking. But when you ask him, be sure that your faith is in God alone. Do not waver, for a person with divided loyalty is as unsettled as a wave of the sea that is blown and tossed by the wind. Such people should not expect to receive anything from the Lord. Their loyalty is divided between God and the world, and they are unstable in everything they do.

JAMES 1:5–8

God never intended for us to be part-time sons. We need to really grab on to the idea that we are children of God and then let Him change the way we think, act, and respond. Our heart should be His, our mind should be focused, and our future transformed.

Don't copy the behavior and customs of this world, but let God transform you into a new person by changing the way you think. Then you will learn to know God's will for you, which is good and pleasing and perfect.

ROMANS 12:2

When we don't connect with the new way of thinking God designed for us, we have trouble understanding what He wants, the work He has for us, and the way it needs to be done. It's almost like we can't understand the language He's speaking.

- -

But people who aren't spiritual can't receive these truths from God's Spirit. It all sounds foolish to them and they can't understand it, for only those who are spiritual can understand what the Spirit means.
1 CORINTHIANS 2:14

- -

The connection between our heart and mind is very strong. Our thoughts lead our heart, and our heart uses that information to act in ways that either bring honor to God or shame to our reputation as Christ followers.

Control your thoughts, ask God to soften your heart, and follow God with a choice to love and honor Him.

Jesus replied, " 'You must love the LORD your God with all your heart, all your soul, and all your mind.' "

MATTHEW 22:37

Thoughts Matter. . . .

★ The Bible can be a great tool to help you bring your thoughts into focus.

★ The things we allow our mind to spend the most time with are the things that will consume our heart.

★ There is a connection between what we think and how our heart responds.

★ Our heart and mind work together to either follow God or a new path that seems entertaining.

★ God wants us to ask Him for help—and then accept it.

★ Our heart should be His, our mind should be focused, and our future transformed.

★ When we don't connect with the new way of thinking God designed for us, we have trouble understanding the language He's speaking.

★ Our thoughts lead our heart, and our heart uses that information to act in ways that either bring honor to God or shame to our reputation as Christ followers.

★ Control your thoughts and ask God to soften your heart.

Fix your thoughts on what is true, and honorable, and right, and pure, and lovely, and admirable. Think about things that are excellent and worthy of praise.

PHILIPPIANS 4:8

CHAPTER 37
TIME TO HANDLE THE TRUTH

Some said he had the gift of a storyteller, but they were just being kind. Lance told lies that were so outrageous that few ever believed him. Some thought he meant to be funny. When asked if he'd gone to the store, he might say he was taken by a government spy association where he was forced to help them overthrow a rival government. The payment for his help was the groceries he brought home. This was how he explained being late. He would follow up every wild story with, "It's true!"

If you were to believe every story Lance came up with, then he'd been to almost every country in the world, made life-changing discoveries, and saved more lives than he could count. He'd even tell you about the time he was asked to join a team going to explore the sun, but he had to decline because he just didn't have enough aluminum foil for his suit. Lance found himself in a place where he could no longer tell the difference between truth and a lie.

Get the truth and never sell it; also get wisdom,
discipline, and good judgment.
PROVERBS 23:23

Truth matters because it brings order to chaos. This can be found in a law that says stealing is wrong. If a person takes something from a store without paying for it, then that person might be charged with the crime of theft. Stealing is not acceptable. If there was no law against it, then anyone could steal anything at any time. That would lead to a lot of chaos.

For Christians there is one place where they can always find the truth—the Bible. The rules are absolute, nonnegotiable, and cannot be broken without a need for punishment.

For everyone has sinned; we all fall
short of God's glorious standard.
ROMANS 3:23

We're supposed to choose God's truth 100 percent of the time, but we *will* fail. Our *sin choice* separates us from God. Fortunately, Jesus did something that changed things forever.

Christ suffered for our sins once for all time.
He never sinned, but he died for sinners to bring
you safely home to God. He suffered physical
death, but he was raised to life in the Spirit.
1 PETER 3:18

This is only one amazing truth in the Bible, but it's one that doesn't change. It is truth even when people don't want to believe it. God gave us a plan, we disobeyed, and Jesus came to the rescue.

If we could come up with our own truth, then truth could change at any time. We would accept something as being true until we didn't like the rule anymore. This never happens with God. God wants us to *tell* the truth. He even says it's proof we're growing up.

*We will no longer be immature like children.
We won't be tossed and blown about by every wind
of new teaching. We will not be influenced when
people try to trick us with lies so clever they sound
like the truth. Instead, we will speak the truth in love,
growing in every way more and more like Christ.*

EPHESIANS 4:14–15

God wants us to *live* the truth. He says this is a way
to honor Him.

*Teach me your ways, O LORD, that I may live
according to your truth! Grant me purity
of heart, so that I may honor you.*

PSALM 86:11

What we say and how we live either proves we
accept and live by God's truth or that we like
stories, share excuses, and deny that God has any
right to be in charge.

Truth that is absolutely true comes from God. Those truths teach us how to spend our time, what to avoid, the value of love, and the need to obey.

Truth matters, obedience is important, and following God is how we find peace in the middle of chaos.

For God is not a God of disorder but of peace.
1 CORINTHIANS 14:33

That's the truth.

Truth Matters. . . .

★ Truth matters because it brings order to chaos.

★ For Christians there is one place where they can always find the truth—the Bible.

★ God's rules are absolute and nonnegotiable.

★ We are supposed to choose God's truth 100 percent of the time.

★ God wants us to tell the truth.

★ God wants us to live the truth.

- ★ What we say and how we live either proves we accept and live by God's truth or that we like stories, share excuses, and deny that God has any right to be in charge.

- ★ Truth that is absolutely true comes from God.

- ★ God's truths teach us how to spend our time, what to avoid, the value of love, and the need to obey.

- ★ Truth matters, obedience is important, and following God is how we find peace in the middle of chaos.

Truthful words stand the test of time,
but lies are soon exposed.
PROVERBS 12:19

CHAPTER 38
SOME STUFF IS JUST THAT IMPORTANT

Kyah was a member of the mythical League of the Well Intentioned. His most recent project was making a priority list. He spent almost two minutes writing down the things he wanted to accomplish. Some things would take years to accomplish, and a few could take minutes if he would just decide to make his bed, put his clothes away, and take the trash out. Kyah knew he had created something special, and he'd get to the list. . .someday.

Many of us have a habit of agreeing that things need to change and then promising change sometime in the future. We don't have to make any changes today, but we feel better believing that someday we'll do something.

We need to remember that while God never changes, we need to. God rescues, but to be rescued we need to relocate to a better place.

For God says, "At just the right time, I heard you.
On the day of salvation, I helped you." Indeed, the
"right time" is now. Today is the day of salvation.
2 CORINTHIANS 6:2

Have you ever heard of someone being rescued
from a river and then going back into the river as
soon as he was rescued? When God rescues us, our
priority should be to learn new ways to live, not go
back to the same conditions that required rescue.

Priorities are usually a list of activities or
interests that are important to you. You may never
find the word *priority* in the Bible, but it does help
us understand what's important to God.

God

Each of us was made for relationship. We have
family, friends, and neighbors. Our best relationship
will always be with God. He made us, takes care
of us, and wants us to consider Him our highest

priority. There is no one like God, and what He says matters.

"Now search all of history, from the time God created people on the earth until now, and search from one end of the heavens to the other. Has anything as great as this ever been seen or heard before?... He showed you these things so you would know that the LORD is God and there is no other."

DEUTERONOMY 4:32, 35

Family

Our family takes care of us and teaches us. No family is perfect, which is why God gave us a command to obey.

Children, always obey your parents, for this pleases the Lord.

COLOSSIANS 3:20

Other Christians

Our journey with Jesus can be hard, but when we walk with others we're encouraged, empowered, and emboldened. We may want to argue with others, but God says, "Instead, be kind to each other, tenderhearted, forgiving one another, just as God through Christ has forgiven you" (Ephesians 4:32).

Forgiveness helps us keep moving forward in our faith walk.

Everyone Else

God's priority has always been people. When you're born, you bring nothing with you, and when you die, you take nothing away. However, the people you meet can be influenced to make God a priority because of what they saw and heard in your life.

Live wisely among those who are not believers, and make the most of every opportunity. Let your conversation be gracious and attractive so that you will have the right response for everyone.

COLOSSIANS 4:5-6

The priorities God wants us to put at the top of our list will always be relationships. We honor Him, obey our parents, encourage Christians, and share the Good News with everyone else. We can use things to help us with these priorities, but things should never move to the top of our list. For instance, we can use our home to show kindness to others, but our home is less important than kindness.

Priorities Matter. . . .

★ We need to remember that while God never changes, we need to.

★ When God rescues us, our priority is to learn new ways to live and not go back to the same choices we were rescued from.

★ Each of us was made for relationship.

★ God made us, takes care of us, and wants us to consider Him our highest priority.

★ There is no one like God, and what He says matters.

★ Our family should be second on our list of priorities.

- ★ When we walk with other Christians, we are encouraged, empowered, and emboldened.

- ★ Forgiveness helps us keep moving forward in our faith walk.

- ★ The people you meet can be influenced to make God a priority because of what they saw and heard in your life.

- ★ The priorities God wants us to put at the top of our list will always be relationships.

- ★ Things should never move to the top of our list.

The LORD has told you what is good, and this is what he requires of you: to do what is right, to love mercy, and to walk humbly with your God.

MICAH 6:8

CHAPTER 39
THE ELECTRONIC DISCUSSION

Silas was a legend when it came to multitasking. He could update his status on social media while his computer game booted up. He could replace batteries in his game controllers while logging in to talk to his friends online. He had a very focused skill set, and friends often looked to him to troubleshoot their electronic issues.

Silas loved his online life because he could stay where things were familiar and comfortable. Besides, he was always close to snacks, and he didn't have to share.

* * *

For his unfailing love toward those who fear him is as great as the height of the heavens above the earth.

PSALM 103:11

* * *

God loves gamers. He loves cell phone users. He loves those who post silly cat pictures on social media. He loves you. That love is unfailing, always available, without condition—and the good news is just beginning.

- -

But you, O Lord, are a God of compassion and mercy, slow to get angry and filled with unfailing love and faithfulness.
PSALM 86:15

- -

God willingly extends compassion, mercy, and faithfulness to all. If you use electronic devices on a regular basis, this includes you—and those you play with, text, and talk to.

Your use of electronic devices doesn't change God's response to you. His love will always be there. God never actually talks about gaming devices, cell phones, or social media, but His love is mentioned often.

There are two issues that God does address that may connect with this discussion, but it could also be applied to many other topics. The first is how we respond to others. Even if we think gaming can be a problem for others, we should refuse the urge to condemn them. This is one of those issues that should be decided by each family.

So why do you condemn another believer? Why do you look down on another believer? Remember, we will all stand before the judgment seat of God.
ROMANS 14:10

The reason this issue matters to Jesus is because electronic devices could take the place of time spent with Him. We could learn the latest route through a gaming castle, or we could learn how to live the way we were intended to live.

"When you produce much fruit, you are my true disciples. This brings great glory to my Father."
JOHN 15:8

Time well spent with Jesus is important. When we spend more time with anything else, we have less time to "produce much fruit." We are often more interested in following something other than the God who created us. What we discover is that making anything more important than God is a waste of time and a missed opportunity.

Jesus thought a lot about the people He was around every day. Only His Father, God, was more important to Him. He loved God. He served people. We are asked to "imitate God, therefore, in everything you do, because you are his dear children" (Ephesians 5:1).

We follow Jesus not to have our own way, but to follow His plan. We follow Jesus to love His people, not judge them. We follow Jesus because He asks us to, and we've accepted. Let's follow. Let's love. Let's serve. When we do that, we may find we like this a lot more than leveling up, grabbing cheat codes, and existing in a game where Jesus has no influence.

God will love you no matter how involved you become in using electronic devices, but will you love and serve God more—or less—the longer you play?

*"No one can serve two masters. For you will hate
one and love the other; you will be devoted
to one and despise the other."*

MATTHEW 6:24

Jesus Matters. . . .

★ God loves gamers. He loves cell phone users.
  He loves those who post silly cat pictures on
  social media. He loves you.

★ That love is unfailing, always available, and
  without condition.

★ God willingly extends compassion, mercy,
  and faithfulness to all.

★ Your use of electronic devices doesn't change
  God's response to you. His love will always be
  there.

★ Even if we think gaming can be a problem for
  others, we should resist the urge to condemn
  them.

★ Electronic devices could take the place of
  time spent with Jesus.

- ★ Making anything more important than God is a waste of time.
- ★ Jesus loved God and served people.
- ★ We follow Jesus not to have our own way, but to follow His plan.
- ★ We follow Jesus to love His people, not judge them.
- ★ We follow Jesus because He asks us to, and we've accepted.
- ★ God will love you no matter how involved you become in using electronic devices, but will you love God more—or less—the longer you play?

Love each other as brothers and sisters.
Be tenderhearted, and keep a humble attitude.
1 PETER 3:8

CHAPTER 40
IT WON'T BE LONG

Jagger's brother and sister were driving him crazy. His family had left on a trip across the state, and it wasn't five minutes before Pippa asked from her car seat, "Are we there yet?" Milos soon followed the questioning. The first fifteen times were tolerable, but Jagger knew there were more miles and minutes ahead of them. The torture from Pippa and Milos would last longer than he felt he could stand. When he asked them to stop, the two giggled and said in unison, "Are we there yet?" Jagger wished they were.

When troubles of any kind come your way, consider it an opportunity for great joy. For you know that when your faith is tested, your endurance has a chance to grow. So let it grow.

JAMES 1:2–4

Some people are really hard to get along with. Some of those people might live in our own home. When they say things that annoy us, do things that frustrate us, or tell irritating jokes, these are moments when God gives us the opportunity to be patient.

It may not sound like an opportunity, but we know that God created us for relationship, which is why we can accept His advice.

* *

Rejoice in our confident hope.
Be patient in trouble, and keep on praying.
ROMANS 12:12

* *

Prayer is always a top-of-the-list suggestion. Whenever we're frustrated, God wants us to let Him hear about it. Whenever we're irritated, He has a solution. Whenever we're annoyed with others, He can relate. With every bit of patience we endure, we are growing.

Patience may start with living through annoying behavior, but when love is added to endurance, we begin to care about the annoying people around us. Patience provides the opportunity to show others the same love God gave to you.

May God, who gives this patience and encouragement, help you live in complete harmony with each other, as is fitting for followers of Christ Jesus.

ROMANS 15:5

People who follow Jesus have some characteristics that show others our leader wants a response from us that is different from what they're used to seeing.

We prove ourselves by our purity, our understanding, our patience, our kindness, by the Holy Spirit within us, and by our sincere love.

2 CORINTHIANS 6:6

Patience isn't something that only applies to people. We can be patient in the difficult circumstances we face, the arrival of news we need to hear, and the annoying words, "Are we there yet?" And like all other things that matter to Jesus, we learn to be patient with other people, life circumstances, and delayed news because He has always been patient with us. He knows how we feel. Sometimes we need to be patient by waiting on God's answers.

Wait patiently for the LORD. Be brave and courageous. Yes, wait patiently for the LORD.
PSALM 27:14

No matter how you look at it, God gives us plenty of opportunity to learn patience. Maybe that's because patience always forces us to choose between frustration and a godly response. If we were never given the opportunity to act in the way God asks of us, then we might not be sure how to respond that way the next time He asks. If endurance is a rubber band, then patience stretches us and allows us to grow in endurance.

When we're waiting in traffic listening to Pippa and Milos ask, "Are we there yet?" or being frustrated by someone who's hard to like, we should choose to love, listen, and learn because the lesson of patience will show up often.

We may not be there yet, but when we keep responding the way Jesus would, we know that it won't be long.

Be patient with everyone.

1 THESSALONIANS 5:14

Patience Matters. . . .

★ Some people are really hard to get along with.

★ Whenever we're frustrated, God wants us to let Him hear about it.

★ Whenever we're irritated, God has a solution.

★ Whenever we're annoyed with others, God can relate.

★ Patience may start with living through annoying behavior, but when love is added to the endurance, we begin to care about the annoying people around us.

★ Patience provides the opportunity to demonstrate the same love God gave to you.

★ People who follow Jesus should show others that our leader demands a different response from us.

★ We can be patient in the difficult circumstances we face and the arrival of news we need to hear.

★ We should be patient with other people, life circumstances, and delayed news because God has always been patient with us.

★ Sometimes we need to be patient by waiting on God's answers.

★ God gives us plenty of opportunity to be patient.

★ We should choose to love, listen, and learn because the lesson of patience will show up often.

I waited patiently for the LORD to help me,
and he turned to me and heard my cry.

PSALM 40:1

SCRIPTURE INDEX

OLD TESTAMENT

Leviticus

19:11 40

Deuteronomy

4:32, 35...232
31:8 77

Joshua

1:9 ....76, 98

Psalms

7:10 167
13:2 148
14:2 207
19:7 196
19:8 197
19:9 197
19:10 198
19:11 198
23:1 190
23:2-3..191
23:4 191

23:5 192

23:6 192

27:1 . . . . 148, 190

27:14 245

31:24 93

34:8 120

40:1 247

42:5–6 79

51:7 120

69:32 142

86:11 227

86:15 237

89:33 58

103:11 236

105:1 101

111:10 36

119:7 209

119:11–12 195

119:105 26

139:16 14

Proverbs

3:5-6 . . . . 77, 179
4:5 37
10:9 46
11:9 54
12:19 229
12:26 54
13:1 134
16:9 24
16:32 153
17:17 54
20:12 100
22:1 . . . . 44, 128
22:24-25 51
23:23 225
25:25 83
27:2 143
28:7 54

Ecclesiastes

4:10 56
4:12 64

ISAIAH

64:8 16

JEREMIAH

29:11 194

29:13 206

EZEKIEL

36:26. 18

MICAH

6:8 235

ZEPHANIAH

3:17 193

NEW TESTAMENT

MATTHEW

3:8	202
5:43–45	149
6:24	240
6:27	70
6:33–34	71
7:8	208
7:11	131
7:26	182
10:42	88
11:28–30	22
13:15	186
22:37	222
28:19	211
28:20	155

MARK

2:17	30

LUKE

5:32	203
6:45	219

16:10 59
21:1–4 88
23:34 149–150

JOHN
3:16 104
3:30 142
5:14 30
5:17 65
8:11 30
8:12 55
8:31–32 47
10:9–11 184
12:26 130
14:15 179–180
14:21 178
14:27 74
15:8 238
15:14 13
15:18 183
16:13 168
16:33 173

Acts

17:27 206
24:16 123

Romans

1:29-32 132
2:4 113
2:15 167
3:23 225
5:3-5 172
5:8-9 116
7:19 113
8:5 138
8:6 138
12:2 35
12:8 84
12:10 160
12:12 . . . . 220, 243
14:10 238
15:5 244

1 Corinthians

1:25 95
1:27 96

2:14 221

6:12 34

9:24–27. 166

10:13 42

13:11. 107

14:33 228

15:33 . . . . 11, 53

16:13 94

2 Corinthians

5:17 20

6:2 231

6:6 . . . . 84, 244

7:10 202

12:10 94

Galatians

1:10 52

5:17 112

5:22–23. 11

6:2 180

Ephesians

2:10	17
4:14–15	227
4:15	110
4:29	84
4:29, 31–32	136
4:32	233
5:1	239
5:1–2	158
6:1–3	129
6:14	50

Philippians

1:6	66
1:10	118
2:1–2	217
2:3	162, 215
2:4	213
2:5–7	215
3:12–14	32
3:14	170
4:6–7	72
4:8	223

Colossians

3:9 46
3:13 210
3:20 232
3:23–24 62
4:2 199
4:5–6 233

1 Thessalonians

5:11 82
5:14 . . . . 86, 246

2 Thessalonians

3:13 83

1 Timothy

4:12 106
6:6–7 125
6:11 176
6:17–19 92

2 Timothy

1:7 152
2:21 119
3:16 155–156

HEBREWS

4:12 200
4:15 124
5:13–14 107
6:19 80
9:14 122
9:22 28
10:36 175
11:6 208
12:7 140
12:14 68
12:15 185
13:5 78

JAMES

1:2–3 173
1:2–4 242
1:5–8 220
1:17 100
1:22 209
2:15–16 214
3:13 38
4:10 146

1 PETER

1:13 218

1:25 156

2:9 188

2:13-14 179

3:8 . . . . 159, 241

3:18 226

4:8 164

4:10-11 102

5:7 70

2 PETER

3:9 205

1 JOHN

1:9 31

2:16 154

3:9 137

3:18 214

4:19 161

2 JOHN

1:5 187

Also Available from
Barbour Books

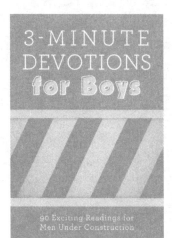

3-MINUTE
DEVOTIONS
for Boys

90 Exciting Readings for
Men Under Construction